PULLING IN THE SAME DIRECTION

A Management Guide for Aligning
Sales and Marketing to Improve Results

Barry Fowell & Chris Behan

1Win Press™ | Los Angeles, CA

Pulling in the Same Direction

A Management Guide for Aligning Sales and Marketing to Improve Results

By: Barry Fowell & Chris Behan

Printed in the United States of America

The authors and publishers have made every reasonable effort to ensure the accuracy of the information contained in this book, but assume no responsibility for actions or results of actions taken based upon its content. If there are errors, please contact us at www.1winpress.com.

Copyright © 2017
Barry Fowell & Chris Behan
1Win Press
www.1winpress.com

Cover and most graphics by Image Design, LLC
www.imagedesignllc.com

ISBN: 1548279021
EAN-13: 978-1548279028

To Ali & Melanie…
With heartfelt thanks and deep appreciation for tolerating clumsy
rough drafts and their clumsier authors.

As well, our sincerest thanks to all of those who helped with the
development and review of this book. Your support and efforts are
much appreciated.

Table of Contents:

Foreword

The disconnect between Sales and Marketing is real in too many companies.

If you have a title including either Sales and Marketing on your business card, the authors are sure that there have been times in your career when you have experienced major frustration with the way both departments work together.

While some disagreements are inevitable, and not necessarily detrimental, wholesale differences in procedures and priorities prevent a company reaching its full potential.

These differences create a philosophical divide between Sales and Marketing which can only be addressed through a better understanding of each department's role in the overall sales process. Digital tools may mask the disconnect for a while, but a lasting solution comes from dialogue and planning.

This book examines each discipline's objectives, motivations and priorities to understand how a disconnect between Sales and Marketing can develop. It then provides a framework which recognizes and integrates the requirements of each discipline into a mutually agreed upon process.

In all candor, this book is not "theoretical" work. We actually worked together at a company prior to the creation of this book.

In Barry's role as the company president focusing on the sales side, and the role of Chris's company managing the marketing activity, we closed much of the philosophical divide between Marketing and Sales by implementing a sales process.

The activity was the predominant reason we grew revenue by more than 500% inside 10 years. We want to share our successful approach with you.

But before we get into the approach itself, some background on each of us may help you better understand our thinking and process.

Barry Fowell – Sales

My name is Barry Fowell. I have been in sales and sales management for over 30 years. In my view, sales is a profession that requires a high level of business acumen to be successful.

A good sales person can be thought of as the sole proprietor of their own small company. They identify customer pain, work with others inside their company's team to find a solution to alleviate the pain, and sell the customer a solution. As the sole proprietor, the salesperson's company profit primarily comes as a result of the sale (commission, bonus, etc.).

This is important because sales people need business skills and sales acumen to bring parties together in the deal. How did I accomplish this when I first started selling? I didn't.

My first sales experience was working for an engineering software company as Technical Director. I moved into sales because I had the potential to earn more money. Besides, I was an extrovert with good technical skills and this was exactly what the role required, or so I was told.

Unfortunately, my ignorance about sales meant a lot of trial and error early in my career. My common, but misplaced, notion that people needed convincing to buy our product resulted in many mistakes.

Initially, I didn't attempt to understand what the prospect wanted, instead peddling our product as a one-size fits all solution.

I showered prospects with as much marketing material as possible, in the hope something in the materials would help my chances of closing a sale. This backwards approach required the prospect to educate themselves about my product.

My opinions about Marketing matched my misguided views on selling. I got leads, but was never able to identify the source. Meanwhile, Marketing spent a lot of money on advertising and trade shows which I didn't believe was helping me to sell. In all fairness to them, I didn't know what to ask for anyway.

Looking back, I wonder how I ever sold anything. Fortunately, I was very process focused, a quick learner and disciplined enough to focus on what worked, while dropping what didn't seem to work.

It was also my nature to want to help people. And I especially enjoyed looking at a prospect's process for potential improvements. As a result, I drifted between my Sales role needing to sell and a facilitator role trying to help customers solve problems.

Ironically, I found my desire to help solve customer problems actually helped me sell. Thus, I got more involved as an advisor to help address customer problems. The more I used this approach, the more successful I became at selling.

My first significant sale started at a tradeshow, where we met a prospect planning to buy from our competitor. He refused us the opportunity to show our product because, "it would take too much effort to change vendors at this late stage".

Despite his refusal, I still called the day after the show and got him talking about what he liked about our competitor's product.

He enjoyed talking about his decision, but conceded there was weakness with the product which alienated his Marketing Department. The product didn't meet their expectations when used for a common task.

Though largely outside the decision, Marketing was not going to get their requirements met. While this was not a deal breaker, it created minor doubt over the purchase. I would not have discovered this insight with my earlier "bury the prospect with information" selling style.

Despite persistent "no's", I managed to get the prospect to meet me the following morning and look at the capability of our system where the competitor's fell short.

Rather than provide him with a generic demonstration, I wanted to show him one specific to his company's products. I hoped the output from this reached the Marketing Department.

For the meeting, we purchased one of the prospect's products at a local hardware store, integrated it into our demonstration and presented it to the prospect. He was impressed by our capability, but the competition still had all the reference accounts for his industry. As a much smaller player, we had none.

Although we didn't have any reference accounts, I had two prospects with whom I had worked. Both were about to buy from us and both were appreciative of our efforts to work with them and improve their processes.

With no other alternatives, I asked both prospects to meet with my new prospect and relate their experiences working with me. The approach was very successful. Two prospects; who weren't even customers, persuaded a third prospect to buy. This was my first significant sale and my first experience with the power of advocacy.

Over time, the more I practiced consultative selling and advocacy, the more successful I became.

And as I moved into sales management, I began to see what it took to be successful managing sales. Ultimately, I distilled it down to 3 key areas:

1. *Enable my sales team to sell using tactics similar to those which made me successful. I wanted a best practices selling methodology.*
2. *Identifying and tracking the interactions between members of the team, others in the organization, and customers/potential customers.*
3. *Eliminate the silo mentality and collaborate with Marketing to ensure we had a productive process which added value at every stage in the sales journey.*

I started addressing the selling methodology by documenting the sales process and continually revising it based on experience.

This document became the handbook for selling our products. Links to resources were also embedded to help sales people navigate the manual and explore selected topics more deeply.

We tracked and recorded customer interactions by developing a rudimentary system using Microsoft Office products, which did what a modern entry-level CRM system does today.

Finally, I worked with Marketing to create a more integrated approach for both disciplines. Many of the ideas we included in that sales management documentation are contained in the pages of this book.

For my part, I co-authored this book to provide you with some effective sales and marketing principles without having to spend 30 years learning them via trial and error.

Chris Behan – Marketing

I'm Chris, and with more than 20 years of marketing experience in both agencies and "client side", my motivation for writing this book boils down to one simple observation:

Marketing philosophy typically values the brand, even if detrimental to short-term revenue.

Sales philosophy typically values short-term revenue, even if detrimental to the brand.

Neither realizes this philosophical difference presents a chasm that hurts EVERYONE…

I've witnessed repeated prejudice from marketers who claim that salespeople just don't "get it" when it comes to both long-term branding and realizing the ultimate vision of the company.

A similar prejudice is frequently mirrored by salespeople who often feel marketing exists just to "make things look pretty".

They assume short-term revenue is always the key for company survival, and that fulfilling the company vision must always play a subordinate role to short-term revenue.

I've often heard salespeople complain about the lack of help they get from Marketing when it comes to meeting the current quarterly target. "Marketing is fixated too far into the future; the real battle is revenue today."

I'd be willing to wager that some of you from either Sales or Marketing, are feeling somewhat defensive after reading the last two paragraphs. Unfortunately, although the sentiments may not always be expressed openly, the underlining conflict is all too common.

If the conflict remains unresolved, company performance over both longer and shorter timescales will suffer.

Both company brand and short-term revenue are important.

Marketing can largely operate independently of Sales when defining the company brand, but Sales cannot effectively operate independently of Marketing to satisfy short-term revenue goals. Here lies the conflict – neither party agrees with the priority of the other party.

Differences between these groups are understandable, given how their performance is typically measured. But in my experience, there were often times where one group pursued actions to benefit their cause – even if it hurt the cause of the other.

Example #1 – Marketing wins! Everyone loses...

A former client (Brand Manager) had to make a budget choice: exhibit at a trade show that customers and high-value prospects attended, or run additional advertising in an already heavy schedule.

Sales insisted that the budget be spent on the short-term sales opportunity presented by the trade show. Marketing favored ad frequency for brand reinforcement. It was never even a contest, the ads were placed and Sales had to skip the trade show.

My client cared more about additional exposure for the brand than Sales getting an opportunity to interact with current and potential customers to generate sales for the company.

Example #2 – Sales wins! Everyone loses...

On the flip side, a former marketing colleague at a technology-branded company, whose products commanded price premiums, was approached by its CEO angrily waving some product literature the company had created.

These materials offered cut-rate pricing as part of a "limited time offer" and also directly compared their product with largely-unknown competitors.

After inquiries, it was revealed that a Sales Manager had made the material to "help close a large deal" so he could achieve their quarterly sales target.

But the flyer was also obtained by customers, who were upset that they did not get this lower price and demanded discounts. The flyer also lost money because it alerted sales prospects that there were also buying options from previously unknown competitors.

In addition to failing to achieve the short-term revenue goal, the flyer also damaged the company's reputation in the market (brand).

CHASM OF DISCONNECT

I have witnessed the chasm of disconnect and its associated complacency, acceptance, and lost opportunities' too often.

The chasm can be avoided (or closed) as long as Sales and Marketing work together to create a sales process which benefits both parties, their priorities, and grows company revenue while still building (and/or protecting) the brand.

To be successful, this gap must be closed through the honest and diligent efforts of both Sales and Marketing. If the chasm is not closed, your entire company risks falling into it.

Ultimately...

It is our goal that this book provides you with motivation and knowledge to help Sales and Marketing work in tandem to close any chasm between the two disciplines or, better yet, keep one from forming in the first place.

SECTION #1

INTRODUCTION

Chapter 1: Background

Many books have been written about business-to-business (B2B) sales and marketing, but few have explored the interdependency between the two disciplines.

This book seeks to do exactly that by viewing sales and marketing in terms of a process - beginning with profiling your target market and ending with your customers providing advocacy to help additional sales.

The concepts outlined in the book result from the authors' extensive experience and success in B2B sales, marketing and most importantly, integrating the two disciplines into a common process.

This book provides the most value for C-level executives, directors and managers who are responsible for sales and/or marketing within a longer-purchase cycle B2B environment.

Such sales are typically higher cost, "non-routine" purchases. For buyers, these purchases often have more risk compared to routine commodity ones. Examples of longer-purchase cycle B2B sales include capital equipment, enterprise software, new technologies, professional services and more.

Although this book targets a longer-purchase cycle B2B market, this does not mean the principles discussed are exclusive to this type of environment. Many of these principles can still be applied, on a case-by-case basis, to other sales and marketing situations.

All people who work in a sales or marketing role should get some value from this book.

Before we begin to consider Sales and Marketing collaborating inside a common process, we need to look at what factors often divide them.

All too often, Marketing and Sales groups have different priorities, different self-assigned metrics, and even different terminology.

This often leads to culture issues between the two disciplines, creates frustration and potentially increases turnover and loss of talent.

One example of different priorities between Sales and Marketing is associated with timescales. When Marketing's priorities are centered around brand building, the goals tend to be medium to long-term objectives, whereas the Sales priorities are frequently about short-term revenue.

Both branding and short-term revenue are important.

Marketing can largely operate independently of Sales when building the brand, but Sales cannot effectively operate independently of Marketing to satisfy short-term revenue goals. Here potentially lies the conflict if neither party agrees with the priority of the other.

Traditional measures of Sales' effectiveness have usually run along the lines of "sales versus target," "pipeline growth" and "close ratios".

In contrast, Marketing's objectives tend to gravitate towards broader measures such as "brand awareness", "target impressions", "exposure frequency", etc.

Both these sets of measures provide value to the organization. But marketing measures are often viewed as requiring too much time before any measurable benefit is realized.

On the other hand, sales metrics are sometimes viewed as being non-strategic and "short-sighted".

Both criticisms have merit since neither focus on both short-term revenue goals <u>and</u> long-term growth.

The philosophy and concepts we explore in this book, seek to align Sales & Marketing, bridging the differences between these two perspectives.

We propose a framework where Marketing adapts to support the shorter-term goals of Sales, while Sales also begins to see the value and accept the longer-term focus of Marketing.

Make no mistake - applying these concepts will come with challenges. Compromise from both disciplines will be required to support a shared vision, and both will need to recognize that neither survives for long without the other.

The goal of this book is to provide you with a basic understanding of both disciplines and their relationship.

Above all, it is intended to equip you with the knowledge to align Sales and Marketing - achieving real and sustainable growth for your business.

Chapter 2: Demystifying the "Black Art" of Sales

Sales is often perceived as a "black art" by those unfamiliar with it. Salespeople are often shrouded with mysticism and their skills deemed almost genetic.

As a result, successful salespeople are sometimes able to hold entire organizations hostage. And companies often view the poaching of "Sales Stars" from other companies as a panacea to cure their own sales problems.

While this may seem to reduce risk, it is only successful a fraction of the time. The success of this approach is usually based on the discipline of the salesperson to follow a process which has worked for them in the past.

If the "Sales Star" depends solely on interpersonal skill, prior contacts or some other aspect of their previous work, then they will probably "flame out" and be unable to replicate their earlier success.

When you treat sales as a "black art", you surrender control of your destiny to a few people within your organization effective at delivering sales revenue.

What factors allow this "black art" mysticism to take root? Understanding this question is key to creating a repeatable and consistent sales process. Gaining this understanding usually begins with exploring how Sales and Marketing groups are viewed in your organization.

Is sales and marketing a common core throughout the whole of your organization, or are sales and marketing separate disciplines, practiced by separate groups that simply share space on the 3rd floor?

If you don't have "Sales" or "Marketing" in your job title, do you understand the role you play to maximize your company's sales?

In too many organizations, Sales is a silo within the company – leading adjacent departments to view it as a "black art". When Sales is productive, there is a grudging acknowledgement of its success.

HELPFUL TIPS:

- Where practical, provide sales awareness training for non-sales staff.

- Create diagrams of your sales process. Use them to educate non-sales employees how everyone in the organization can influence sales.

  This helps the whole organization adopt a common language describing the sales process. It also provides everyone with an understanding of activities and responsibilities in each stage.

  The authors held similar courses several times and never experienced a situation where a non-sales employee expressed doubt about their ability to influence sales.

An underperforming Sales team, however, finds no support from adjacent departments when it comes to evaluate and possibly change salespeople.

In a silo culture, salespeople can be viewed as overpaid prima-donnas. They are seen as people who bend, or even break, the rules other departments have created to ensure the company runs smoothly.

In turn, Salespeople view these same rules as restrictive or, at worst, rules created to make selling as difficult as possible.

You may have worked in a company where some form of a silo mentality is reality. How did this situation develop? Essentially, it results from a lack of understanding about the sales discipline.

BEWARE:
The Sales Skill or Process "Hoarder"

Sometimes, Sales "stars" view their own sales process as "black magic" and try to avoid sharing their insights or other information about how they sell.

This is often symptomatic of a misplaced belief that their job security is based on this knowledge, and therefore they are the only person who should possess it. These people are often more concerned with their own success than that of their team.

You must make sure that you provide a reassuring environment so that they feel comfortable sharing the "secret of their success", instead of hoarding it like a tribal witch doctor. (Thus the "black magic" metaphor.)

A lack of understanding of sales perpetuates the myth that "black magic" is in play, and that it is practiced by slick wizards with mystical persuasive powers.

Sales silos typically create frustration, high staff turnover and disappointing performance. Sales growth is difficult until you shed the divisions and align sales and marketing within a common process.

When adapted to sell your product or service, this process will enable you to grow your revenue and help focus your entire organization on aligning responsibilities to grow the company.

This is a key reason the curtain needs to be lifted - so that all stakeholders can see the true nature and effectiveness of sales within the company. Sales success is not due to some mystical personality trait or skill.

Successful and sustainable sales are the result of a well-defined and uniform sales process – whether provided by the individual salesperson or management.

As explored in detail later, this sales process includes specific and uniformly-described steps, techniques and measures that are used across the organization.

When defined by the organization, a sales process enables results to be duplicated by a greater number of people and frees you from dependence upon a few "stars" for ongoing sales results.

This sales process takes new contacts through a journey to becoming a customer. The book describes a sample process successfully applied in numerous organizations to sell into B2B accounts with longer sales cycles.

We don't claim to have a monopoly on what all sales processes look like. The process will vary depending on the industry and product or service sold. The sales process used in this book is for illustration purposes, but will provide valuable insights into developing and deploying yours to optimum effect.

Ultimately, your own Sales and Marketing teams should be the ones leading development of your specific sales process for a few crucial reasons:

- *Salespeople should be experts about "how" and "why" customers buy, and on the processes they go through to evaluate and make purchases.*

- *Marketing should be experts in crafting messaging relevant to the "why" put forth by sales, and communicating it at the appropriate "where" and "when".*

- *People tend to trust things they are part of, active participation from both groups in the development of the process establishes dialog and overall "buy-in" to the final process.*

For the purposes of our example sales process, this book sets specific terms to bring a common language to the overall process:

Contact – *an unqualified individual. Someone from the target market who has yet to be qualified (i.e. determine whether they can buy our product or service.)*

Lead – *a qualified contact. Someone who could purchase if they are persuaded our offering provides a better, cost justifiable, way of performing a task.*

Prospect – *a lead who is in an active buying cycle and has a budget to purchase.*

Customer – *someone (usually a prospect) who has purchased from us.*

Advocate – *someone (usually a customer) who helps us sell to others inside or outside their company.*

Chapter 3: Branding vs. Sales Marketing - different branches on the same tree

From college studies well into their careers, most marketers are inundated with books, exercises, case studies, and strategies centered around one of the most glamorous and high-profile areas of marketing – "brand building" or "branding".

The aspiration of many marketers is to be the architect of the next big cultural brand. And why wouldn't they aspire to this end? They've been indoctrinated for years that this is the "Holy Grail" and what marketing is all about.

The marketing degrees many colleges offer are taught through the college of liberal arts – not business. This alone begins to shape the content and resultant perceptions of many people interested in becoming marketers.

College marketing curricula are most often shaped through the eyes of "brand-building". This is likely influenced by the fact that branding principles change relatively slowly when compared to other disciplines within marketing, and that branding is perceived as more "glamorous" than other marketing disciplines.

But what may be the largest influence is professors are often more comfortable working in the theoretical and qualitative "branding" aspects of marketing.

Since "direct", "content-focused" and "sales support" aspects of marketing are more quantitative, accountable and oft-changing, they are viewed more as a sales discipline than a marketing one.

Brand-building also provides an opportunity for marketers to tie themselves to a legacy – just look at Steve Jobs, Henry Ford or Jeff Bezos.

Compare those icons with a lowly embedded marketer who is engaged with "sales marketing" and responsible for supporting the Sales team with revenue generation.

Many branding traditionalists would envision this role as sitting in an office poring over detailed content outlines, direct campaign plans, endless spreadsheet analysis, and database culling.

BRANDING VS. SALES MARKETING AT UNIVERSITIES

Though slowly changing, branding still tends to be the default mode for marketing curricula at universities due to two reasons:

1. Many college professors tend to prefer the "theoretical" world of branding, since the broad principles are based on human behavior.

2. Sales marketing techniques often vary by industry and current status of potential customers. As a result, they are harder for colleges to frame within generalized syllabi.

Students are usually best served by taking internships to experience sales marketing techniques as they apply in a specific industry.

All of these activities produce quantifiable results (i.e. accountability) which directly affect the revenue line of the income statement.

This is a foreign and uncomfortable concept to many branding-focused marketers who would most likely associate this type of role more with accounting or statistical analysis than marketing.

However, a thorough understanding of branding and brand-building should never be construed as negative or useless. Quite the contrary, it provides a foundation for understanding many of the disciplines within marketing.

It also helps to reinforce the message that every audience touchpoint ultimately influences the brand. A single-faceted skillset is a mistake for marketers because, there are comparatively few opportunities in the market for branding "specialists".

All marketers need to embrace principles on how their efforts not only affect their brand, but also how they support (or fail to support) sales efforts.

Ultimately, a marketer could do their job developing "brand awareness" and "brand preference," but if no one actually purchases the product, the organization will not survive, no matter how great its brand perception.

Conversely, if an organization has a level of sales to sustain itself, but has low brand awareness and preference, can it realistically grow long-term?

While both branding and sales are important to an organization, the brand cannot exist without sales, and sales can only grow to a certain point without growing the brand.

Chapter 4: Aligning Sales & Marketing to Produce Results

The initial step in aligning efforts of Marketing and Sales groups is to establish candid communication and active dialog between the two disciplines.

This will eventually serve as the basis for trust between the two disciplines and will help them focus on the objectives that serve the organization as a whole – producing measurable and uniformly accepted results.

This starts with both groups working together (lead by Sales) to identify and map-out what the organization's sales process looks like as a whole.

It includes identifying the various stages of the process, the common characteristics of the constituents within that stage, typical stage duration, sales objectives for that stage, and the criteria of what moves constituents to the next stage.

Though some salespeople may resist "generalizing" the sales process within their organization, this process is not intended to be highly-descriptive for every sales opportunity ever encountered.

It is meant to provide general directions that cover the vast majority of how the organization sells.

As such, it is strongly recommended that this sales process be reviewed and approved by key members of the Sales team for both functional accuracy and internal "buy-in".

The creation of a sales process map facilitates candid and honest discussion between Sales, Marketing and organizational management, and allows each to gain a more accurate perspective in terms of how their offering is typically sold.

By documenting the sales process, each stakeholder will get a better understanding of its strengths and weaknesses.

Agree on common terminology

Once the general sales process has been mapped-out, the next step is to adopt terminology which has "standard meaning" between the sales and marketing functions.

Leaving fungible language promotes individual interpretation, facilitates miscommunication and provides understanding "gaps" which can cloud the meaning of results.

> Seems like "Common Sense" but...
> *Uniform Language & Terms = Uniform Understanding*

This can reach a point when managers have a difficult time making a decision because the definition of key terms fluctuate based on the team member and no one is operating from the same set of definitions.

This selection of terminology should primarily be driven by the sales process map.

While drafting or selecting these terms, keep in mind that they do not necessarily need to translate to the world outside of your organization.

It does not matter how someone outside the organization interprets the terms, as long as your team has a clear understanding of them.

It doesn't even matter whether you label a contact with a specific phase "prospect," "suspect" or "marshmallow." If your entire Sales and Marketing teams associate a uniform definition with those terms then they should serve well for monitoring the overall process.

Use this terminology as the basis of Sales and Marketing integration

Start with a high-level overview of your sales process and how you measure it. This is key to removing subjectivity and cloudiness associated with salespeople operating under their individual models.

Eliminating the individual models will enhance the effectiveness of typical sales management activities such as pipeline planning, reporting, gap/problem identification, day-to-day management, and training.

The second result of this activity is common terminology for a sales process map that serves as a sort of "Rosetta Stone" for your organization, allowing Sales and Marketing groups to both literally speak the same language.

This uniformity of language is less common than you might think. Disparities between Marketing and Sales, based on this seemingly small issue, can cut deeply when an organization's size reaches a certain critical mass.

Candid dialog and uniform terminology will be imperative as Marketing and Sales begin to review the sales process map to determine how Marketing can help Sales move contacts through each phase of the sales process.

SECTION #2

AN INTEGRATED SALES & MARKETING PROCESS

Chapter 5: Process Introduction

For the purposes of discussion within this book, we will introduce a "sample" sales process to illustrate concepts, terminology and general goals for each stage of the sales process.

The process is intended to be used for illustration purposes only. While large portions of it will match your business model, it will most likely need to be customized to fit your industry and specific business.

The most important endeavor in this process is to actively and honestly explore and document your sales process/model. This will enable you to understand how it works and help you better support its various phases by understanding their objective and dynamics.

The resulting diagram can also be used to train current/new Sales team members to make them effective more quickly.

(If it fits with your model, it will also help you be more effective when evaluating and integrating CRM tools such as Salesforce® Act!® and others. Key principles about using CRM tools are addressed elsewhere in this book.)

As discussed earlier, the crucial facets of this process involve working with appropriate Sales team members, marketers and other stakeholders to ensure the elements of the sales process model are accurate, standardized and uniformly understood.

To ensure there is understanding of the terms in this book, they are defined as follows:

Overall Segment or Industry – This is the overall area in which you are selling your product/service.

Industry-focused offerings are those which are focused on a specific industry, such as aircraft engine parts, medical equipment manufacturers, automotive testing services, etc.

Segment-focused offerings, however, are not usually defined by a certain industry, but are generally focused towards a certain segment (or job role) within organizations.

Common examples would be CAD software (for design engineers) or independent auditing services (for internal accounting departments).

NOTE: Based on experience, most offerings will gravitate towards ultimately being targeted at a certain segment (or job role). Even the most ubiquitous products (toner, paper clips, etc.) are usually purchased by certain people within an organization – ranging from a purchasing department to an administrative assistant.

Do not be surprised when your industry-focused offering also comes with a segment-focused subcomponent. If you already know this, or even discover it during your sales modeling process, it will actually enable you to be more effective sooner.

In Appendix B, you will find a general "flowchart" – illustrating a sample sales process. This is meant as a visual reference for you as we describe the process.

We included it to help you more fully understand the concepts and nomenclature used throughout this book. We recommend that you refer to it frequently while reading subsequent chapters.

This flowchart will aid an understanding of the journey a person makes from contact to advocate in our example sales process.

SUGGESTION:
Referring to the Sales Process example in Appendix C will help you better understand descriptions and chapters.

As introduced in Chapter 2, these stages are:

Contact – *an unqualified individual. Someone from the target market, who has yet to be qualified (i.e. determine whether they can buy our product or service.)*

Lead – *a qualified contact. Someone who could purchase if they are persuaded our offering provides a better, cost justifiable, way of performing a task*

Prospect – *a lead who is in an active buying cycle and has a budget to purchase*

Customer – *someone (usually a prospect) who has purchased from us*

Advocate – *someone (usually a customer) who helps us sell to others inside or outside their company.*

These terms were selected because they are descriptive to most people familiar with marketing and sales.

However, as we stated earlier, your terms will be up to you, as long as Marketing and Sales can both agree on them, and more importantly, what each term means.

The traditional "funnel" - an over-simplified and limiting metaphor

The traditional funnel has been used for decades and is very good at illustrating the attrition rates at various stages.

It also effectively shows the way that leads percolate down the funnel until some of them become customers. It may be an attractive graphic for a sales presentation to non-sales management, but that is about all the value it provides.

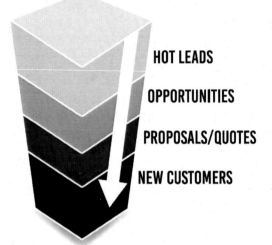

HOT LEADS

OPPORTUNITIES

PROPOSALS/QUOTES

NEW CUSTOMERS

The traditional funnel fails to adequately describe any sales process which is more complex than the one implied inside the funnel. It also fails to describe what each stage means, the goals at each stage, and ignores any effects that can be exerted on the process by Sales and Marketing.

The funnel doesn't describe how Sales and Marketing interact at different parts of the process. Nor does it represent the "ownership" of different stages in the process as the "contact" progresses along the journey to becoming a "customer".

The funnel assumes a top-to-bottom flow. In reality, individuals can churn in one segment of the funnel and can actually flow backwards in some cases. The funnel also implies that there is only one way in and one way out.

As noted, the funnel fails to adequately describe the external sales and marketing stimulus needed to progress contacts through to customers.

It also ignores how Marketing adds new contacts and nurtures them through the process. The traditional funnel doesn't address potential hand-off of leads to Sales, and the efforts by Sales to close as large a percentage of these leads as possible.

The best way to capture the real complexity of your sales process is to think of it as a set of individual funnels as illustrated in Appendix B.

Within each of those funnels, Sales and Marketing both have individual and collective responsibilities, to transition the contact/lead/prospect/customer to the next funnel within the overall sales process.

The traditional sales funnel has been expanded into five distinct funnels with transitions in between. We believe that this approach better explains the process by which contacts are qualified as leads, activated as prospects, closed as customers, and energized as advocates.

The fifth funnel represents the activity to nurture customers to become advocates and become catalysts for repeat business. This approach also explains more deeply the ownership roles and the inter-relationship between effective Sales and Marketing groups.

Marketing tends to focus more on contact generation, lead qualification and nurturing (often through multiple touch points) and plays a supporting role in activating leads into prospects.

Sales tends to spearhead lead to prospect activation and largely-owns closing prospects to customers. Finally, both Sales and Marketing play very important roles in energizing advocates.

Chapter 6: Contact Generation

While the ultimate goal of the sales process is to develop customers and advocates, the process must initially begin by gathering a large pool of people with potential to purchase your product or service.

This is the primary objective of the initial phase – "Contact Generation".

At this point, gathered contacts are not leads and many of them will not become leads. (The process of filtering the contacts to identify leads will be described in the next chapter).

When beginning contact generation, it is often a better practice to cast a wide net to ensure you are capturing as many feasible contacts as possible. It is better to include contacts that will later be filtered out by Marketing than to miss a potential customer by narrowing your focus too quickly.

When you become more experienced at contact generation, the profile or common characteristics of a typical customer will likely begin to crystalize. This will help you to adjust criteria during contact generation to become more efficient.

> **RECOMMENDATION:**
> Cast a wide net for contact generation to avoid being too narrow and accidentally filtering out potential customers. With experience, you can tighten your filters.

As your sample size (customer base) increases, you will also be better able to identify patterns such as job title, company size, job function, and more, which have a stronger potential to buy your product or service. Ongoing adjustments, as your customer base grows, will also help increase your conversion ratio from this phase to the next.

These adjustments will enable you to tighten your initial criteria, targeting and acquisition tactics to better-fit the customer profile. This more targeted activity will increase your measure of efficiency (conversion ratios) and reduce waste throughout your process.

Profiling your Target Market

There are two critical, and one optional reason for you to make an honest and descriptive profile of the target market/audience for your offering:

- Develop highly-effective communications messages that promote the benefits of your offerings through the lens of the audiences' concerns, and motivate them to act

- Identify the most effective and efficient methods (and media) to communicate that message

- *(Optional)* Provide insights for future product development and refinement to make it more appealing/competitive within this segment. (This is not covered in the book)

The Sales team (or Sales management) is usually the best source of information both on your target market and the objectives for this contact identification phase. As such, they should be involved. This is not an activity left purely for Marketing to accomplish alone.

When exploring the facets of the target audience, marketers' end goals will be best-served if they obtain "demographic-style" data from the team as well as insights into the "psychographics" of the intended target audience.

This includes additional information about the audience's identification/evaluation process. Sample factors include:

- *Perfunctory demographics*: industry, job title, job role, company size, company product

- *Catalyst/motive/pain background*: themes/goals/problems influencing target audience in relation to your offering - based on industry, job role, company type

- *Product identification/evaluation*: how does the target audience typically identify potential solutions, where do they get their information (i.e. media content and consumption), who are industry opinion-leaders, immediate qualifiers/disqualifiers for our type of product

---

UNDERSTAND YOUR TARGET MARKET

We cannot stress enough, the importance of correctly identifying and targeting the right market for your product.

Early in my career, we sold a product which we believed was ideal for Automotive OEM's and Tier-1 Suppliers.

We had some success, but frequently came across the perception that our product was better suited to the Aerospace industry.

We targeted the Aerospace industry and received feedback that our product was better suited to the Process industry.

Essentially, we made the mistake of targeting a generic product at multiple industries without addressing the nuances and terminology unique to each one.

It wasn't until we really researched the needs of each sector, and made minor modifications to the product, that we got real traction for the product in multiple industries.

As part of the background on catalysts or motives, Sales management (or team members) should be able to describe at least the three, main market pressures driving your target to make changes in how they do things pertinent to your offering.

Note that you should think of the target as both an individual and as a company. Although people, not companies, buy your products, the company profile influences, and often determines, whether the individual can buy.

EXAMPLE: CAE SOFTWARE

Decision Maker: Chief Systems Engineer
Pain or Motivator: Pressure to produce more efficient systems at lower cost and development time.

Influencers: Systems Engineers
Pain or Motivator: Need for greater insight and accurate predictions of how systems behave under various operating conditions.

Influencers: IT Department
Pain or Motivator: Concern over compatibility and standardization across different departments.

The correct people to receive the message must also be identified. In many organizations, there may be related targets that need targeting with slightly different messages.

You could try to make contact with all of these different individuals by using different messages that appeal to each of their needs.

It may be more pragmatic to select just one key target and identify the associated contacts during the contact qualification phase.

As a rule of thumb, you should first target the individual most likely to be the decision maker (e.g. the "chief systems engineer" in the example) rather than the end user. There will be more chance of success if the decision maker sees the benefits in your message and pushes it "downhill" by involving the reporting engineers.

It is a harder sell to target the engineers and expect them to push your value "uphill" to management.

However, if you are unable to define your audience's pressures or motives with a reasonable level of confidence, then you should acknowledge that a more in-depth understanding of the market is needed. Effective contact generation relies on a thorough understanding of your target market.

Crafting your Message

The initial impetus to profile your intended audience, begins by gaining an understanding of their motives relative to your offering. You must also gain an understanding of how these pressures align with, or overlap your offering's overall value proposition, by thoroughly understanding the benefits of your product or service.

The areas of commonality (or overlap) between the target audience's pressures/motives and your value proposition provide the basis for your promotional communications messaging.

The intent of your messaging is to gain attention and drive response, by leveraging market drivers amongst your target audience. This messaging will be most effective if you propose a feasible solution that relieves relevant pressures affecting their activities.

If there is little or no overlap between your target audiences' pressures and your value proposition (benefits), then your value proposition should be rethought, or a new audience should be targeted based on your current value proposition.

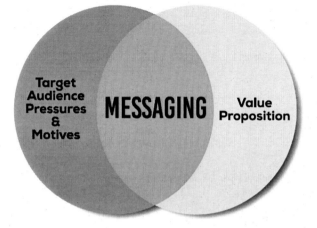

Once you have identified the overlap between the audience's market pressures and your value proposition, this understanding can be used for outbound message development.

When developing outbound messages, it is important to view your messaging through the prism of your audience's goals and objectives, and not through your own goals as a seller.

Your audience is trying to solve their own problem – not yours. As a result, there is not enough time or attention for your audience to absorb, process and translate messages that do not speak directly to their particular needs.

Ideally, your key messages should identify overlapping points succinctly, using language/terminology common to the audience in a manner that gets attention and is easy to assimilate. This is one of the areas where talented marketing communications folks really prove their worth.

Typically, it is best to distill your messages into a prioritized hierarchy that is efficient in communicating various levels of detail – depending on the level of interest.

- *Primary message*: the single message almost everyone must receive and understand
  - Must address the pressure, and position your value proposition as a solution
  - Typically addresses highest, or most common, market pressure

- *Secondary messages*: additional message(s) that some should receive and understand
  - Includes additional pressures and how your offering addresses them
  - 1-2 additional messages

- *Proof points*: provides some general substantiation for above messages (optional)

Note that if your offering is sold in different industries/segments, the pressures and resultant messaging may vary accordingly.

Most marketing communications media used for contact generation is unable to deliver more than a few messages and proof points simultaneously.

Luckily, this is of little consequence, as most people are only able to process a certain amount of information at a single time.

As a result, the precise message should focus on the needs and motivators of your target audience given the limited bandwidth of the media and finite attention your message will receive.

Ignore the temptation to dilute your message.

Ultimately, the goal for contact generation is to get your future customers to "raise their hand". Simply creating a positive feeling across a broader spectrum of people without enough motivation for your target to respond is antithetical to your end goal.

Many people believe broadening (read: diluting) their message is somehow safer and will enable them to proportionally widen the audience to which their message has meaning.

This is a double-edged sword. Broadening a message's appeal can also reduce its motivational capabilities among the target audience. If someone responses to a diluted message, it is likely that the quality of contact will probably be lower.

There is a contrast between these two approaches. Focusing your message is more a direct marketing approach intended to identify contacts, while the broadened approach is often misconstrued as "building brand awareness".

This broader approach is less effective for what we are trying to accomplish at this stage. Thus, you must be careful to maintain consistency and not dilute the message to the point where it becomes largely ineffective for the goals of contact generation.

Hopefully, your efforts to profile your target market from earlier in this chapter have provided information to support the statement.

Nonetheless, the points in the box are two of the most difficult concepts for many to grasp – mentally and emotionally.

Since messages are only interesting to those for whom the benefits are relevant, you should be careful about your own personal feelings about your messaging.

In order to create messaging that motivates your audience, you must put yourself in their position.

CRAFTING YOUR MESSAGE – KEY POINTS:

1. You are not your target audience.

2. Your offering is more interesting to you than it is to your target audience.

3. Your audience is interested in their problem(s), not your offering.

This was one of the two primary purposes for profiling your target market. Understanding their role, their pressures and their market dynamics helps "put you in their shoes".

This allows you to communicate with them about the benefits of your offering through the lens of their problems and concerns.

Secondary Message Testing

There are circumstances where it may be possible to test different messages to your audience. When possible, message testing enables you to identify which of your messages most motivates representative samples of your target market.

In turn, this lets you adjust your messaging as time passes. Message testing is recommended when:

- Your message development process has identified more than one secondary benefit message that would be motivating to your target audience

- The benefit messages are complimentary to each other and not mutually-exclusive *(as your audience may be exposed to both messages)*

- Overall outreach effort is large enough to accommodate a test of multiple messages *(if you're only running a small effort, testing multiple efforts will more likely dilute your communication than provide a realistic test)*

- Your outreach media/campaign structure enables you to accurately measure responses to different messages

Since your primary message (broad benefit-based) should be consistent, the messages that get tested are ideally *secondary messages.*

This leaves your larger, "brand position" intact while helping to determine which of your supporting messages matters most to the audience.

Savvy marketers sometimes also factor-in these findings when refining or developing new products.

Driving action and response.

Having developed a message that reflects benefits the target is seeking and motivated them to learn more, you now need to provide a clear call-to-action. This call-to-action outlines the next steps necessary to learn more about those benefits.

These actions range from asking the audience to make a phone call, visit a website, watch a video, download promotional materials, or a host of other options. These factors may even include some of your own criteria for transference to the next phase of your sales process.

No matter what your call-to-action may be, its promised end-result should offer some perceived benefit to your audience in terms of solving the issue(s) addressed via your messaging.

APPLIED EXAMPLE: CAE SOFTWARE

Industry: Automotive Manufacturing
Decision Maker: Engineering Director – Powertrain Systems
Pains or Motivators:
- Operate optimally across all ranges of vehicle drive cycles
- Package the componentry into smaller footprints
- Ensure the powertrain is transferable/scalable across vehicle platforms
- React quickly to changes in body styling constraints
- Conceive and evaluate innovative new concepts

Influencers: Powertrain Systems Engineers
Pains or Motivators:
- Need to design systems and components in less time
- Increased pressure to reduce prototyping costs/cycles
- Need to share data across multiple suppliers

Gatekeepers: IT Department
Pains or Motivators:
- Concern over standardization across departments
- Worry about computer security and shared data
- Concern about difficulty of integration into IT platform

Primary Messages: "Our solution will enable you to…"
- Quickly design and accurately evaluate performance across vehicle drive cycles and operating conditions
- Rapidly react to changing design constraints and evaluate new concepts

Secondary Messages: "Our solution will enable you to…"
- Reduce the need and amount of required prototypes
- Securely provide design data to vendors in a common format for easy use

---

Delivering your message

Having profiled our target market and crafted our messaging accordingly, we also need to identify the most efficient and effective methods to deliver the message.

The identification and filtration of potential contacts consists of two primary areas: active marketing communications outreach and inbound marketing infrastructure.

Active Communications Outreach

The relationship between your active outreach and marketing infrastructure is analogous to the relationship between ocean currents and coral.

Like our marketing infrastructure, ocean corals are static and do not hunt, they simply trap/catch bits of food, driven by the oceans' currents, that flow through their branches.

It is up to the oceans' currents to determine the direction of the flow and the density of food contained within the flow. Our active outreach mimics the source and flow of water (contacts) to our marketing infrastructure.

Thus the objective of active outreach is to direct and/or funnel potential customers into your marketing infrastructure (discussed in previous section) for capture and processing.

Ultimately, the goal is to create water flow(s) (outreach methods) that optimize the density of "food" (contacts) flowing into our coral (capture methods).

Our active outreach challenge is then to deliver as many quality contacts to our infrastructure for the least amount of expenditure/effort.

ACTIVE MARKETING OUTREACH	MARKETING INFRASTRUCTURE
ADVERTISING	WEBSITE
TRADE SHOWS	LANDING PAGES
SEARCH ENGINE MARKETING	SALES MATERIALS
PUBLIC RELATIONS	INBOUND CALL CENTER
DIRECT MARKETING, ETC	

The following are typical communications outreach methods:
- Advertising (various media, sponsorships, listings, social media, PPC campaigns)
- Public Relations (articles, reviews, speaking opportunities)
- Search Engine Marketing (targeted content, social media, referral links)
- Trade Shows/Events (attendance, exhibition, attendee/exhibitor list purchase)
- Direct Marketing (email and mail campaigns, outbound call centers)

"Effective" vs. "Efficient" Communications Media

It is often assumed that the terms "effective" and "efficient" marketing media can be used interchangeably, when they are actually different in a sales marketing environment.

From a sales marketing/sales process perspective, one of the most "effective" means of communicating with potential customers is via a direct personal dialog. This approach requires hordes of salespeople making telemarketing calls to broad industry-based lists.

But given the high cost of trained sales personnel and low "hit rates" on phone dials, its efficiency is very low and its cost to reach even a few people is prohibitively expensive.

In contrast, one of the most "efficient" means of communicating with your target audience is advertising in trade media.

EFFICIENT COMMUNICATION | EFFECTIVE COMMUNICATION

MARKETING Social Media Websites / Landing Pages
Sales Literature   Technical Materials
Search Engines / PPC   Trade Shows
Trade Advertising   Sales Cold Calls
Public Relations   Personal Presentations
Telemarketing / Call Centers **SALES**

LOWER COST / EXPOSURE | HIGHER COST / EXPOSURE

While advertising can reach large numbers of your target market quickly and at a relatively low cost per exposure, it only gathers a few seconds of attention and thus can only communicate 1-2 points of your messages.

It also depends on the reader taking action in order to learn more about your offering.

Filtering inbound contacts is one area where a solid marriage between Marketing and Sales groups pays dividends and marketers can earn their stripes.

Savvy marketers will strive to find a balance of media that is "efficient" in terms of cost and communications effectiveness - leveraging their most "effective" (and expensive) sales marketing assets (the sales team) to make them more efficient.

Optimizing the flow of contacts

In order to be successful, and best measure how well the outreach methods are yielding results, we must do both pre-outreach planning and measurement, and post-outreach measurements, to gauge the results of our efforts.

Pre-outreach Evaluation & Targeting

All evaluation during the planning phase should ideally be performed through the lens of your target audience.

Generalized measures adapted from the "branding" (and/or consumer) world will not provide the level of detail necessary for you to make management-grade decisions regarding your sales planning.

When reviewing measurements from potential media outlets, traditional broader measures such as overall traffic, CPM and others must be adjusted by removing those who clearly do not fit your target profile, as they are of little or no direct value to you.

Going through this exercise as part of planning, enables a pre-execution view of the cost per exposure for your target audience. It also provides a valuable first step in an overall cost and efficiency measurement for your entire sales process, from the initial generation of contacts through their ultimate purchase.

Post-outreach Measurement

Measuring responses from active outreach activities also benefits us in other ways. If you know which contacts are generated from which activity, you will be in a position to determine the most cost efficient activities.

As you move forward through the process, these measures also allow you to compare other costs at each phase, including a cost per customer by outreach type. This provides insights into your sales process and allows you to adjust and improve your customer acquisition rate.

For clarity, it is recommended that each outreach method (and media) be accompanied by an inbound tracking mechanism discussed in the call-to-action earlier.

Common inbound tracking mechanisms:
- Discrete phone (or 800) numbers (by method, by media, by campaign)
- Discrete website landing pages (by method, by message, by media, by keyword)
- Database/CRM tracked (manual entry based on trade show, cold call)
- Vendor-provided tracking (CTR reports, bingo cards, lead sheets)

Often, one particular type of outreach will have a high yield of contacts at a lower cost, but very few of those contacts eventually become customers.

In contrast, another outreach method may yield fewer contacts at a higher cost, but most of those contacts eventually become customers. The costs and ratios of each will ultimately tell you which is more effective. But you need to have measurement from the start in order to determine which ultimately benefits your sales process more than the other.

The tweaking of these various outreach methods (and testing of new ones) is a constant process that requires ongoing attention, measurement and adjustment.

Inbound Marketing Infrastructure

Marketing infrastructure can be considered any element of your marketing that does not proactively reach out to your target audience, but instead, relies on your active communications outreach to "be fed" and gain exposure.

Typical examples of infrastructure include websites, online landing pages, brochures, and inbound call centers that primarily rely on another mechanism to deliver viewers/traffic.

As mentioned earlier, an accurate analogy for the relationship between your infrastructure and active outreach would be the relationships between coral and ocean currents.

The objective of your marketing infrastructure is two-fold. The first objective is to effectively communicate your messaging to the inbound contact, in a manner and at a sufficient level of detail, that helps them classify/categorize your offering, and that also gives them an idea of whether or not your offering would be of benefit to them.

The second is to efficiently capture the contact information of these people, much the same way as coral captures its food. This capture could range from a direct phone call from the interested contact to opting-in for future outreach communications from your organization.

At a minimum, the level of information captured should be enough to establish an ongoing line of communication with them. This information can be captured using a variety of measures, including website sign-up forms and subscribing links to phone numbers.

Typical information-capturing mechanisms:
- Online forms (websites, landing pages)
- Phone numbers (800 numbers)
- "Bingo Cards" (old school - from trade magazines)
- Personal (from personal contacts at trade shows)
- Purchased industry lists (filtered based upon your audience profile)

> ## CAPTURING CONTACT INFO: A TRADE-OFF
> Less required information = quantity > quality
> More required information = quantity < quality

When crafting any information-gathering mechanism, you must keep in mind that there is a paradox between the amount of information you request and the number of respondents captured.

Requesting more information will usually result in fewer respondents. The responses, however, will be of higher quality and will allow you to segment/customize your communications messages based on that greater detail.

At the other end of the scale, the less information gathered will typically result in higher capture rates but the subsequent quality of dialog will be lower and more generalized.

Although you will have basic information, you will know comparatively little about your captured audience. The ideal situation is to strike a balance, or compromise, between the two variables.

This will enable you to both capture a sufficient number of contacts to feed your sales process, and to capture enough information to provide tailored messages that keep your captured contacts interested.

Managing Captured Contacts

To take the next step in our filtration process, we need to track the sources of contacts and continue dialog with them. Without this, much of the effort and resource we have invested to generate the contacts will be wasted.

Therefore, representatives for both Sales and Marketing should work together to develop processes and reporting structures that ensure the goals of their respective departments are met.

- *Marketing*: Ability to track contacts to a level of detail that provides decision-grade information to marketers in terms of the outreach method performance (cost and volume). Also need the ability to monitor the life cycle of these contacts in order to determine the ratio of contacts that convert from one stage of the sales process to the next.

- *Sales*: Ability to filter these contacts based upon key factors identified by the Sales team (i.e. propensity to buy), so that resources and efforts of the Sales team are leveraged as efficiently as possible. (In other words, you don't want Sales reps chasing "junk" contacts or those who have a very low propensity to purchase your offering.)

About Commercial CRM Systems…

CRM (Customer Relationship Management) systems are vital to track your contacts through the different stages of the journey until, in some cases, they become customers.

They also provide a centralized reporting source if your sales resources are geographically-disbursed.

However, as the numbers of users and possible permutations of sales situations multiplies, these systems make the standardization of sales terminology and concepts mentioned earlier in this book even more critical.

CRM is such an important tool in today's sales and marketing process that we devote a separate discussion to it towards the end of the book.

Chapter 7: Lead Identification

At this stage, you have successfully profiled your target market, crafted and communicated your message and convinced potential buyers to provide their contact information in response to a message and value proposition they think will benefit them in some manner.

However, the value of your message and their resultant response was based on the audience's understanding that your product or service can benefit them directly.

Given this positive response, it's very important that Sales and Marketing work together to nurture the interest. This interest may signify that you have a "lead" rather than "contact".

Why is this important? A potential, future customer has responded to you and signaled their interest in your product or service. You need to nurture them until you can confidently re-categorize this contact as a lead.

To ensure we are still approaching this from a uniform perspective, we should begin by reviewing the definitions that were introduced earlier.

Contact – an unqualified individual. Someone from the target market, who that has yet to be qualified (i.e. determine whether they can buy our product or service.)

Lead – a qualified contact. Someone who could purchase if they are persuaded that our offering provides a better, cost justifiable, way of performing a task

By definition, leads are a subset of contacts, and this definition implies, that not every contact can (or will) become a customer. Here is the key value of separating "lead identification" from "contact generation".

Since the process of identifying a lead from a larger pool of contacts shares some common elements with the original contact generation process, companies will sometimes believe they are being more efficient by simply combining the two phases into one – lead generation. In this way, every new contact is also a lead.

However, combining contacts and leads into a single category of "leads" usually undercuts the very efficiency it was intended to create. One of the principles we noted earlier was a salesperson's involvement in the sales process tends to involve higher levels of cost. In most organizations, salespeople are a finite resource.

Thus, if you assume all contacts should be sent to the Sales team, then you have to assume every contact generated is of high enough quality to not waste the costly time of a salesperson.

Simply forwarding unfiltered leads to the Sales team quickly becomes a bottleneck in your process. Nothing disrupts the harmony between Sales and Marketing more than contacts sent to Sales under the guise of leads, when they are either unfiltered or of poor quality. This approach wastes a valuable resource – salespeople's time.

Under these conditions, Sales eventually stop following-up the leads provided by Marketing. Subsequently, Marketing will become frustrated that their leads are not being followed up by Sales, your organization will miss opportunities that might reside in that pool, and your sales will suffer as a result.

To avoid this dysfunction, we must acknowledge that, for whatever reason, not every contact will buy from us. Some just don't fit our profile. They may have requested information on our products to educate themselves about market trends or other reasons.

CONSEQUENCES OF NOT FOLLOWING UP ON LEADS:

We have come across, and even been involved in, numerous examples where leads forwarded to Sales are not followed up.

There are usually three high level reasons why this happens.

- There is no effective sales process in place
- There is a process but the execution is poor
- Marketing generates more quality leads than Sales can handle

Having too many good quality leads can change opportunities into spoilage problems – depending on the buying cycle and patterns of your audience.

The situation needs to be addressed by either adding sales resources, or by allowing Marketing to become more involved in lead screening.

The first two reasons, if not resolved, will seriously affect the company's ability to sell, and will create serious morale issues especially within the marketing team.

The situation where Sales stops following-up leads often occurs when the performance metrics of the sales and marketing teams are not common ones.

Marketing may be focused on increasing the number of leads generated, but have no quality standards in place.

Sales may have over ambitious lead qualification expectations and may decide that all the leads they receive from Marketing do not meet the minimum quality standards.

Regardless of who is to blame, the sales process needs to be examined, and probably modified, to ensure everyone is working synergistically.

Standardizing Criteria for Leads vs. Contacts

Since sending all contacts to our Sales team isn't necessarily our best option, the most efficient way of qualifying or disqualifying them should be left mostly to Marketing.

Having Marketing spearhead the process of lead identification does not mean Sales is uninvolved, nor is the sales function relieved of any responsibility for this phase.

Quite the contrary, much like the earlier contact generation phase, Sales and Marketing must cooperate in order to determine uniform (i.e. agreed upon) standards for criteria that elevate/differentiate a "lead" above a mere "contact". These criteria can usually be classified into two types:

- *Profile-based criteria*: This includes a variety of criteria that describe the contact including identified target company, job role, and department. It's likely that most of this profile-based information will have been identified during the contact generation phase.

- *Behavior-based criteria*: This includes action(s) taken by the contact indicating a personal (or professional) interest in your product or service. This interest can range from visiting a trade show presentation, to responding to an outreach campaign, to downloading promotional or technical materials, to making repeated website visits. Whatever the behavior, the individual is signaling an intention to understand more about your product or service.

Any quantity or combination of the above (or other) criteria can be grounds for elevating a contact to lead status if Sales and Marketing agree that the criteria is appropriate.

This agreement benefits Marketing because it helps them plan, adjust and measure their outbound campaigns to more efficiently drive responses fitting the criteria. The agreement also benefits Sales because the criteria identification process, and adherence to a standardized set of criteria, virtually guarantees a level of quality for the inbound leads.

However, these standards should not be considered perpetual and an additional agreement between Sales and Marketing to review the criteria for potential revisions and/or improvements is necessary.

Exception to the Process – Salesperson Override

Though the process strongly dictates that Marketing owns contacts and Sales owns leads, there will likely be instances where salespeople may feel a certain contact (or group of contacts) offers a high-probability sales opportunity.

In this situation, Sales will likely want to directly follow-up with the new contact rather than simply "leave them in the pool", with the rest of the contacts, until they meet the set criteria for a lead.

This can be accommodated in the sales process by allowing Sales to view all contacts as they are generated. Sales can then directly elevate identified contacts to lead status for direct sales qualification, without waiting for the contact to reach lead status on their own.

However, salespeople must be disciplined to either upgrade the contact to lead and apply the appropriate agreed upon process steps for its status, or leave the contact in its current state.

This allows Marketing to continually nurture the contact to get them to raise their hand in response to lead identification efforts, thereby helping them reach lead status based on standard measures.

Identifying Leads out of Contacts

Lead identification is a marketing-driven activity, designed to repeatedly reach out to the contacts in the database, to persuade them "to raise their hand," in a manner that differentiates them from the larger pool of contacts.

Having Marketing cultivate contacts from leads is relatively efficient. As described in the previous chapter, marketing communications tend to provide a lower cost per exposure in comparison with higher cost sales-based communications.

As a result, requiring a sales-type follow-up with all generated contacts becomes impractical and highly inefficient.

EFFICIENT COMMUNICATION · EFFECTIVE COMMUNICATION

MARKETING · Social Media · Websites / Landing Pages · Sales Literature · Technical Materials · Search Engines / PPC · Trade Shows · Trade Advertising · Sales Cold Calls · Public Relations · Personal Presentations · Telemarketing / Call Centers · SALES

LOWER COST / EXPOSURE · HIGHER COST / EXPOSURE

The process of identifying a lead is very similar to contact generation, with the exception that you have already captured the person's details. Having the contact details means that the marketing message or offering can be more tightly focused.

There are several marketing methods available to help identify a lead from a base of contacts. Some of the more common methods include:

- *Active outreach campaigns* (email, postal mail, etc.): This is the practice of marketing running routine outbound campaigns to the database (or list) of contacts. These campaigns typically offer some incentive as a reward for response (discount, white paper, video, webinar, event, etc.).

In today's email campaign systems (VerticalResponse, Constant Contact, etc.) each contact is monitored for the type of action taken in response to the campaign (email opens, click throughs, etc.). The responses to these are then tracked against the lead criteria, and for marketing purposes, for response rate comparisons.

- *Advertising campaigns*: Repeated responses to advertising campaigns from a single contact, across media with different messages and offers, tends to indicate an elevated level of interest. This is different from a one-time respondent to an ad, who should be treated as a routine contact.

- *Trade events/presentations*: Attendance at a specialized presentation, or visiting a trade show booth, likely indicates a high level of interest and, in many cases, could even be pre-screened by your show attendees. In highly-niche markets, attendance at technical presentations often indicates the area/type of work your contact is engaged with.

- *Repeated website visits/downloads*: Depending upon your level of sophistication, website visitors can now be individually tracked, and their visits to your website and other online properties (blogs, landing pages, etc.) automatically entered into many, commercial CRM systems. Repeated visits to your website, and downloads of materials from your site, also indicate a high level of interest in and/or potential application of your product/service.

- *Telemarketing/call centers*: in certain circumstances, it might make sense to employ a call center to help identify leads from a large pool of contacts. Please note this is different from having your Sales team contact this pool.

Telemarketing is a lower cost/higher volume option, that makes sense in certain situations. An inside person or outside center, working from a script, can screen a number of contacts a day. This resource is less costly than an experienced salesperson qualifying contacts.

Any number, or combination of these methods for identifying leads can be used. They can be weighted differently, based on the perceived efficacy, to yield leads that meet the agreed-upon criteria set forth by Sales and Marketing.

As contacts repeatedly raise their hands in response to these methods, the likelihood of them being a legitimate lead increases.

These methods also enable Marketing to segment the contacts within the database and target messaging based upon their particular motive. Much of this information is derived from the initial collaboration between Marketing and Sales groups to identify the target market, audience and their potential dynamics. This also enables Marketing to test different messages against different audience segments and thereby optimize responses based upon these factors.

If you are currently using a more advanced CRM system (such as Salesforce), there are modules available that can automate a scoring process based upon criteria that you set up within the system. It would be worth the time to investigate such an option to make the monitoring and follow-up from Marketing and Sales more efficient over time.

At this point, it is worth mentioning that we assume anyone contacting your company directly via phone or email and specifically asking for more information about your product/service, automatically bypasses this process. This individual is already considered a lead and receives immediate and personal follow-up.

Converting Contacts to Leads

In practice, Marketing's decision to convert a contact to a lead and pass the lead to Sales is largely a provisional one. It is results from the Sales team follow-up directly with the potential lead, that determines if the decision on whether the change in status is valid.

This means that the salesperson is using their most valuable resource (time) to interact with this potential lead. As a result, salespeople need to be very discerning when deciding whether to work with this contact (now a lead) or whether they should be left with Marketing to be nurtured with further marketing campaigns.

In determining whether to accept the change in status, the salesperson contacts the individual to establish potential for, and willingness to, change from the way they do things currently. If the salesperson doesn't believe they have a lead, then the contact returns to pool of contacts on whom lead identification continues.

> *Sales' bandwidth should never influence conversion from a Contact to a Lead or vice versa.*

This decision should be made based on the salesperson's assessment of the lead. Ideally, if the lead is not a quality one (and is therefore still a contact) the salesperson should work with their existing leads, prospects and customers and trust Marketing to do its job of lead identification.

When leads are sent back to contact status, it is up to both Sales and Marketing management to review this group in aggregate, to re-evaluate current lead criteria, and identify potential common shortfalls in the predictive capability of those criteria.

This review should include the identification of standards/criteria, that must be met, before contacts downgraded from lead status, are eligible to be re-classified as leads again.

Sales bandwidth should never be the determining factor in whether a contact can be a lead. Demoting leads based on a salesperson's bandwidth dangerously assumes the sales potential is largely perpetual.

It also assumes that the contact will neither be approached by competitors, nor will actively seeking alternatives to your offering. This could potentially lead to sales opportunities being lost because a salesperson was simply too busy to build a dialog.

If members of the Sales team are overburdened, Sales management should keep in mind the best interest of the organization as a whole, and should review alternatives to sales resource allocation that enable the organization to respond to potential opportunities in a timely manner.

Salesperson follow up with leads

Once a salesperson receives notification of a possible lead, they need to quality the lead and decide where this change in status to lead is justified. This can be done as a face-to-face visit, or more likely, via phone call. This process may even take several interactions over a number of days.

Unless the salesperson has contacted the potential lead in the past, this will be the first interaction between them. As such, the salesperson needs to make a judgement on the potential of the contact as a future customer.

This means they have to begin thinking about the endgame and consider questions the buyer will need answers to before committing to a purchase.

- *Lead's view*: "Does my business 'pain' open me to change how I do things today?"
  Salesperson view: "Can they articulate their pain and will they change the way they do things?"
- *Lead's view*: "Can change be economically justified?"
  Salesperson view: "Is there a valid value proposition?"
- *Lead's view*: "Which vendor should I work with to make the change?"
  Salesperson view: "Will they make the change with me?"

BUYER'S QUESTIONS

In a B2B environment, the ultimate buyer's question is usually based on some form of financial benefit. The buyer needs to be able to see a clear financial reason for making the purchase.

This financial reason is less common in B2C transactions, where the buyer is often motivated by the positive feelings they get from making a purchase.

These are general observations. Several years ago, I purchased a snow blower as a B2C transaction. I justified the purchase based on the cost of a snow ploughing service for one season.

Though I must confess to the delight I experienced using my new toy on the first snow of the winter.

In some circumstances, the buyer may change the order of these points– choose the vendor and work with them to justify the investment.

Going from initial contact to discussing the buying questions is not a trivial step. The process will continue, not only through the contact-to-lead process, but also though the lead-to-prospect stage.

This doesn't mean, however, that the salesperson should not be considering the strategy on how to answer these questions at the earliest stage of the customer journey.

During the telephone call/visit the salesperson needs to establish the potential, and the willingness, for the contact to change from the way they do things today.

This is arguably the key phase in the sales process. They are a lot of moving parts to this initial conversation, including:

- What does the contact understand about our products?
- What prompted them to contact us?
- Do they understand the pain we address?
- Do they understand their pain?
- What is the company doing to address this pain?
- Can they purchase a solution or initiate the buying process?

The importance of his key phase in the sales process should not be subject to a chance conversation. The activity requires a prepared script.

This doesn't mean that the salesperson follows the script verbatim, but it does mean that there are strong guidelines to help the salesperson get the most out of the call.

A typical contact script has a number of objectives:

- *Introduce* you and your products to the contact
- *Establish* whether, after a set process, the contact might purchase your product
- *Identify* any alternative contacts that the original contact might recommend

Any call over 5-10 minutes in duration is probably too ambitious at this stage.

The contact script should contain the following components:

- *Introduction* – purpose of the call, use and business benefit of your product
- *Confirmation* - of the contact's title, job function (probably an open question!) and applicability as the appropriate contact
- *Qualification* – number of open qualifier questions to establish individuals who might purchase. These should be documented as part of the script (and your CRM system) so that the salesperson can select appropriate ones and record responses during the conversation. Examples of open qualifiers are:
  - How would you describe your role in the organization?
  - What problems are you currently experiencing?
  - Why is this an issue?
  - How does that affect the process?
  - What happens when you encounter this issue?
  - Who owns the pain?
  - Has the need been triggered by a particular activity?
- *Agreement* - to a specific follow up action (e.g. a follow up call)

Even if the contact is very interested, the salesperson may not get to the all the qualifier questions in the first call. It may be necessary to handle the qualification over several calls.

Keeping your contact database clean

While it makes some sense to treat non-responsive contacts (i.e. ones who have not raised their hand since being loaded into your CRM system) as dead, and routinely clean them out of your system, this is probably not the best option.

As long as the relative cost to keep marketing to them is low, a better option is to remove them from your routine outbound marketing activities but leave them in the CRM system.

Though these contacts may seem to offer no immediate sales potential, the landscape tends to shift over time. Job and role changes have become relatively routine, along with their resulting spheres of influence.

These changes could impact the contacts' ability to purchase (or influence the purchase) of your offering in the future. If the cost to continue active marketing outreach to these contacts is prohibitive, it may be advisable to simply reduce the number of active outreaches to them.

Consider creating infrequent, specialized outreach campaigns, that have a goal to keep them exposed to your message and/or reconfirm their existence and interest. The only contacts we might recommend purging from your systems are the ones whose contact information has become invalid.

But that approach becomes risky if the contacts have any notes or details about them on file, which would be lost in a purge. These notes would be valuable if the contact becomes active at a later date.

In conclusion

At this point, we have identified leads from a larger pool of contacts and routed them to Sales.

In turn, Sales have reviewed and/or contacted the leads and have either sent them back to the pool of contacts for continued outreach and aggregate evaluation, or have confirmed their status as genuine sales leads.

Our next step is to further explore these leads to determine their possibility to be prospects.

Chapter 8: Qualifying Leads and Generating Prospects

The sales cycle now has a population of leads which have the potential to become customers. At this stage, it is helpful to review the definitions of "lead" vs. "prospect" for contrast and a better understanding.

Lead – a qualified contact. Someone who could purchase if they are persuaded our offering provides a better, cost justifiable, way of performing a task.

Prospect – a lead who is in an active buying cycle and has a budget to purchase.

Ultimately, what separates leads from prospects is their inherent status of being active.

A lead has only just begun to show interest or develop a general awareness of a problem or opportunity for improvement. They might casually investigate options, but a prospect is "active" in their engagement of their particular issue, as well as developing views on this issue.

Active refers to the current intent defined by the decision-maker's:
- Engagement and awareness of their problem
- Understanding of the current pain and the implications of the status quo
- Active identification and evaluation of potential solutions

Active engagement also typically requires a prospect to have available budget resources and a commitment to making a beneficial change. (A commitment a lead has not made nor is willing to make yet…)

Prospects will likely be at varying states within their purchasing process.

Thus, Marketing and Sales groups will need to be cognizant of this in terms of messaging and expectations. The three states typically look something like this:

- *Investigation*: Lead is aware and has a general definition of the problem they are trying to solve (or what they are trying to achieve) and is investigating potential solutions they believe might help accomplish that objective (also referred to as a "solution set")

- *Evaluation*: Lead has formed a solution set and reviews the attributes of each in terms of the detailed specifics of their problem and goals, along with any potential constraints they might be facing

- *Selection*: Lead has formed a preference towards a solution and is mentally identifying potential processes in which that solution could be deployed to achieve their objective(s)

The duration of each of these can be measured in minutes or months – depending on a variety of dynamics, ranging from complexity, to cost, to organizational processes.

At this point, the salesperson needs to partner with the potential buyer. The goal of this newly-formed team is to solve a problem. How does the potential buyer address their challenge or improve upon their current way of accomplishing a task?

This partnership is the key used by the salesperson to convert leads (a person who might be open to buying our product) to become a prospect (someone in an active buying cycle).

In the previous chapter, we noted three questions the buyer (and salesperson) will need to answer before committing to a purchase.

Lead's view: "Does my business 'pain' open me to change how I do things today?"
Salesperson view: "Can they articulate their pain and will they change the way they do things?"

The salesperson seeks to answer the first question by establishing the potential, and the willingness for the lead to change from the way they do things today. This discovery phase is addressed through qualifying topics:

- Purchase motivation
  - What triggered the need/pain (particular activity, incident, market pressures, etc.)?
  - Who owns the pain or has the duty to address it or improve current methods?
  - Why are they prepared to spend money (no internal expertise, need quick solution, etc.)?

- Purchase resources
  - Are funds available and are there any constraints (amounts, timing, etc.)?
  - Who owns the budget, or who will be allocating the resources, and what is their role in the purchasing process?

- Purchase process
  - How does the company buy products/services such as yours?
  - Who is involved in the decision and/or implementation processes?

Lead's view: "Can change be economically justified?"
Salesperson view: "Is there a valid value proposition?"

A valid value proposition cannot be identified until the aforementioned discovery phase has advanced to a point, that enables Sales to identify how the solution addresses the buyer's pain or improves their process.

However, the salesperson still needs to provide preliminary pricing information if needed, and have a good idea about how they are going to present a strong value proposition. We will go into the process of creating a value proposition in much more detail in the next chapter.

Lead's view: "Which vendor should I work with to make the change?"
Salesperson view: "Will they make the change with me?"

As the prospect continues the journey to becoming a customer, their focus shifts from "what should I buy?" to "whom should I buy it from?" This is particularly applicable if your offering contains products and/or services that are similar to those that may be offered by competitors.

The selling of consulting and professional services often falls into this category since the prospect is technically buying something that will not clearly differentiate itself until after the purchase has been completed. As a result, a strong value proposition is needed to support these decisions to justify the investment in your offering versus those of your competitors.

As you can see, getting from lead to prospect is an extension of the customer journey. It involves:

- A growing awareness of the changes that need to happen – Question 1.
- Better awareness of solution proposed – Question 1.
- Creating a powerful value proposition – Question 2.
- Budgeting funds to make the change – Question 2.
- Developing trust between the lead and salesperson – all questions, vital for Question 3.

At this point, the prospect is probably following a similar journey with several vendors. The salesperson must build credibility and begin to differentiate their solution.

The aim is to make the prospect feel comfortable with the solution (i.e. mitigate their inherent feeling of risk).

Under these circumstances, the salesperson must have empathy with the prospect and be trusted to fairly represent their own solution.

The salesperson's credibility in the eyes of the prospect is essential to the bonding which needs to occur so both parties continue to investigate a solution to the prospect's pain.

Marketing's first roll during this phase – helping Sales build credibility and differentiate

To help support Sales within this phase, Marketing must shoulder a role that continues to differentiate as well as build credibility.

Depending on the nature of the offering and the potential buyers' purchasing process, Marketing must act as a narrator by communicating messages reinforcing the strengths of your offering, contrasting it with competitive offerings and mitigating concerns/potential objections from the buyer's perspective, or any combination of these.

The range for these types of activities can be very broad. Examples include:

- Boilerplate-type of messages/support materials that address common concerns
- High-level points of differentiation found with other customers
- Highly-customized pieces specific to the prospect or opportunity

Credibility provides a foundation for your next steps.

Prospects need reassurance that your salesperson understands their market and challenges. The prospect also expects the salesperson to be credible when tailoring and presenting their solution to address their challenge or process improvement.

Prospects often want more than just a good relationship with the salesperson to commit to purchasing. They may also need to gain a sense of confidence (or mitigated risk) with proof in the form of seeing the potential solution in operation.

Often, successful salespeople maintain a mental portfolio of brief stories or anecdotes regarding their offering, and are able to use them during initial discussions with prospects to position the offerings as a potential solution.

Really disciplined salespeople are always trying to increase their portfolio by seeking out additional examples from customers, internal staff and other sales team members.

If a higher (or more formal) degree of information is needed, references and more detailed examples of previous implementations that were successful, can be an effective approach to build credibility.

This approach often uses testimonials or brief case studies to indicate how others have benefited from your product.

It is important that your examples (or references) should overlap as many factors of the prospect's situation as possible. These factors can range from similar industries and functions to a common problem shared by both your customer and the prospect.

The more you can overlap the attributes of your example with the current situation of your prospect, the more confidence they'll have.

> **SUCCESS STORIES**
>
> Success stories are a very powerful way of building credibility for your product or service. They should be used as a natural part of the dialogue and not as part of a formal presentation.
>
> A good story has a link, or trigger, which prompts the story (e.g. "It's interesting that you raise the topic of .... we encountered a similar situation at .... and we ....")
>
> The use of success stories demonstrates the salesperson's empathy and understanding of the lead's industry and challenges - demonstrating the applicability of the offering to address challenges like those being experienced by the lead.

This type of reference selling is very powerful and you should leverage every opportunity to gain advocates, testimonials, case studies and other useful information.

The topic of advocacy has its own process stage and chapter later in this book.

Differentiation – what makes your offering different and better

Another objective at this stage is to create a clear differentiation between yourselves and the competition. Though it may be tempting to simply create a blow-by-blow feature (or attribute) comparison between your offerings and those of your competitors, the most meaningful differentiation is usually customer-centric.

It is important that you place yourself in the customers' position and identify (from their perspective) the important benefits your offering delivers that your competitors' does not. You should also identify how your offering delivers the benefit better than your competitors'.

Expressed graphically, it would look something like this:

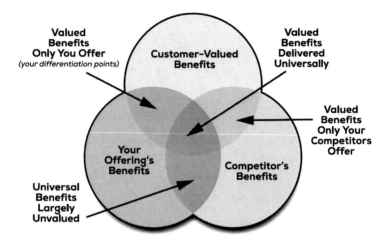

Many of these benefits can often be identified from customer conversations and should be tied-in with your overall value proposition if one has been formed at this point.

Once the prospect becomes aware of valuable benefits offered by you but not by your competition, then specific features and functions not tied to a value category become less important.

Marketing Resources versus Practicality

A classic tension that frequently forms between the sales team and marketing is when it comes to the development of materials. The guidelines for allocating development resources can frequently be distilled down to this:

Marketing Team – often seeks to develop fewer tools that address the most common themes across broadest audience.

PRO: Tends to be more efficient in terms of resources – covering general and common customer issues and concerns.

CON: These materials often hit the target in some area, but rarely score a bullseye in terms of addressing concerns for any particular customer. This often forces the salesperson to cover the gap (or worse, try to create their own materials).

Given the resources required, the level of customization will depend on a variety of factors that include, purchase cycle timing, product category or type, average transaction size, the relative expectations of your industry segment, etc.

(Much of this is covered during the "defining the audience and market" discussed earlier in this book).

> Policies on customization of marketing materials for potential customers should be determined by Sales and Marketing Management – based on market conditions, practices and expectations.

To use a health care example, if you manufacture artificial replacement joints for implant, (high prospect volume, low transaction size), creating generalized marketing materials (for doctors and patients) would probably be sufficient to support your sales team.

However, if you sell CAT Scan machines (low prospect volume, high transaction size), your sales team may be better-suited to have materials customized for prospects (hospitals, universities, large medical practices, etc.).

The key job for those managing Sales and Marketing groups is to develop a uniform policy (or guidelines) for the development of marketing materials.

These guidelines must take into consideration the aforementioned market factors, as well as internal (and in some cases external) marketing resources and capabilities.

Bear in mind, as the decision to rely on custom materials increases, these factors must not only be viewed in terms of your current volume of prospects, but you must also consider what resources will be required to follow your guidelines and produce materials, at the volume of prospects required to meet your target sales levels.

Marketing's second role – keeping your offering in the leads' solution set

While the bulk of our discussion has focused on leads that have converted to prospects and how to move them forward through the sales cycle, most of your "leads" will not necessarily convert to "prospects" on the first pass.

This may be due to any number of reasons, but awareness of our offering must still be "maintained" amongst them for future opportunities. This is best suited for Marketing.

Based on the definitions of "lead" and "prospect" we use in this book, the differences between them (budget, active purchase process), will usually be due to timing.

Typically, a lead simply doesn't have budget when we connect with them, or hasn't been able to clearly define the problem yet, or other similar issues that will most likely resolve themselves in the near future.

Since it is a better use of the Sales team's time to continue focusing on prospects and sales rather than leads, the best option to handle these leads is to simply leave them in the marketing pool for continued outreach and dialog activities.

The outreach messages and methods can either be similar or identical to the ones used to identify them in earlier chapters, or more customized based on gathered knowledge.

Decisions on the appropriate approach depend on the level of sophistication in your CRM system and on the expertise of your in-house marketing team.

Continuing to touch these leads on an ongoing basis helps our offering maintain its position as an "identified potential solution" once the lead's aforementioned timing issues are resolved.

These leads would then be reactivated at a later time based on a variety of actions – depending on standards agreed to by Sales and Marketing management, such as:

- *Lead-initiated*: lead reactivates themselves by directly contacting the salesperson
- *Lead-initiated*: lead responds to an outreach effort (or a preset number of outreach efforts) and receives a status call from salesperson
- *Sales-initiated*: salesperson contacts lead for a status call according to a preset time interval
- *Sales-initiated*: salesperson can call lead for any reason to check status

Aside from the lead reactivation, it is up to Sales and Marketing management to determine guidelines for when a lead should be considered inactive, dead or otherwise removed from outreach activities altogether.

Moving prospects on to the next phase

We have put the leads back into marketing circulation and have the Sales team working with prospects who have decided to make a change and allocated a budget. All we have to do now is convince them to buy from us...

Chapter 9: Closing the Sale

Prospect to Customer

From the previous chapter, a prospect is an individual who has resources and is in an active buying cycle. Assuming the salesperson has accurately identified the prospect, then they have resources and are committed to selecting and moving forward with a solution.

Since your prospect has made this decision and allocated the needed resources, their decision is now "which solution?" Touching on the questions first noted in Chapter 8, no sale can occur until the buyer and salesperson are able to answer their respective versions of three core questions:

1. *Buyer view*: "Does my business 'pain' open me to change how I do things today?"
   Salesperson view: "Can they articulate their pain and will they change the way they do things?"

2. *Buyer view*: "Can change be justified?"
   Salesperson view: "Is there a valid value proposition?"

3. *Buyer view*: "Which solution should I work with?"
   Salesperson view: "Will they make the change with our solution?"

At this point, the salesperson is now spending an increasing amount of time on this and other prospects.

Therefore, it is very important that impromptu audits are conducted using qualifier questions.

These audits are often handled by Sales management who ask the Sales team questions about the specific opportunity similar to the following:

- Who owns the pain of their current situation or process?
- Who else is involved in the decision?
- How does the company buy products? Has the need been triggered by a particular activity?
- Why are they prepared to allocate resources (budget, personnel, etc.)?
- Are the resources currently available?
- Who owns or controls those resources?

Uncertainty at this stage, on any of the qualifier questions above, can potentially derail a sale.

If the salesperson has a good understanding of the answers, it is time to spend more time focusing on the value proposition (salesperson's core sales question 2) and how to convince them to select our solution (salesperson's core sales question 3).

Tuning the Value Proposition

A value proposition is a perceived or tangible value a customer can expect after buying a product or service.

Many deals stall because prospects were unable (or unwilling) to create internal value propositions needed to justify purchase resources.

As such, we recommend that your salesperson takes the initiative on this effort and does not leave the future of the potential sale to the whims of the prospect.

In the early stages of our sales process, we utilized a broad value proposition to position ourselves in our contact generation efforts.

This later value proposition is an adaptation of that broader version. The result should be a sharper focus on the original value proposition to address the prospect's specific situation.

SALES MANAGEMENT ACCOUNT AUDITS

I've sat on both sides of the table during an account audit. As a salesperson, I didn't enjoy the experience. All too often feelings of frustration surfaced. "Why is this meeting necessary?" "Does my manager not trust me?" "I understand this account better than anyone!"

During one such meeting, the manager asked "who besides your contact is involved in the decision to buy?" I had been reassured that the decision was the prospect's alone. Fortunately, my manager was persistent and strongly suggested that I contact a customer in another department, who was a strong advocate of ours.

The feedback from the advocate suggested that the prospect didn't have the authority to purchase, and we were introduced to the real decision maker, with whom we closed the deal. Following this experience, I still didn't enjoy the meetings, but I did see value in them.

As a sales manager, I considered these account audits as a partnership activity with the sales team. I used audits to ensure we understood as much about the account as possible to maximize our chances of closing deals. I cannot confirm that every salesperson enjoyed them, but I believe every salesperson found them beneficial.

It should be viewed in terms of an "applied value proposition". The broader version is made more granular and adapted to address the prospect's particular needs by outlining how our solution performs against these needs.

This value proposition should be communicated to your prospect in a formal document that contains the following elements:

Element #1: Overall issues (pain points) and causes

This first element communicates the pain points and their source. It positions the challenge which needs to be addressed.

Business pain can come from many sources. Examples include: lack of skilled workers, quality concerns, excessive manpower costs, legislation, excessive time to market and product costs when compared to those of a competitor. The source or combination of sources will likely be unique to each situation.

Earlier in the book, we proposed that change is driven as a prospect or lead asks the question "Does my business pain motivate me to change the way I do things today?" These pain points and their cause(s) need documenting in Element #1 of the value proposition.

Element #2: Implications (costs, risks, inefficiencies, etc.) of doing business in the current way

Here, we document how each of the pain points noted in Element #1 affect the performance of the prospect's program, operations or the overall company. This is basically documentation of costs to the prospect of maintaining their current status quo. This will serve as the baseline for later comparison.

Earlier we listed the following examples:

- o Legislation (compliance/insurance costs)
- o Lack of skilled workers (how is this problem being addressed and what is the cost)
- o Quality concerns (damage to brand/market image)
- o Excessive manpower or rework costs (how many hours at what cost)
- o Excessive time to market (missed opportunity)
- o Product costs (poor competitiveness).

Element #3: Your proposed solution and related costs

This element documents your solution and outlines the expected cost(s) of its implementation, ongoing usage and other related costs.

Element #4: Expected benefits to be realized by adopting your solution

This element explains the benefits that your prospect can anticipate receiving in return for selecting and implementing your solution.

Depending on the nature of your prospect, motives for purchase and other factors, these benefits can vary widely (savings, reduced risk, speed, confidence, etc.).

However, it is strongly advised that, as much as possible, they be presented in some sort of quantitative format with financial units of measure being preferred.

Element #5: Overall Expected ROI

This element is a summary of the financial benefits minus the cost of implementation associated with investing in the change. Expressed as a mathematical equation, it would look something like this:

Expected ROI (Element #5) =
Expected Benefits (Element #4) +
[Cost of Status Quo (Element #2) - Proposed Solution Costs (Element #3)]

This detail demonstrates you have a clear understanding of the prospect's situation, need for a solution, applicability of your solution, and an idea of how your solution will perform in terms of their measures.

This level of detail is often enough for this stage, but you should be aware many companies will review the investment in your solution against financial accounting measures such as payback period, return on investment (ROI), Internal Rate of Return (IRR), etc.

If these measures are to be used to help assess the impact or performance of your solution, it is strongly recommended that the salesperson understand this, as soon as possible, in order to craft a value proposition that best addresses these measures.

Proof of concept / test drive

Unless your solution provides intuitively obvious and very favorable advantages (or you have no competition), you could be asked, depending on your solution and the nature of your business, to take part in some form of feasibility or trial performance evaluation.

If there is a competitive offering in the mix, this often takes the form of a solution-vs-solution face-off. If there is no competitor (or if your competitor is the status quo) it usually takes the form of a trial period, feasibility study, pilot program, test drive, or similar variation.

The specific motives for these exercises varies slightly, but they usually circulate around two core drivers – determining the applicability of considered solution(s) and mitigating perceived risk of implementing the considered solution(s).

Keep in mind, these factors are often grossly underestimated in the B2B segment because they are frequently viewed from a B2C perspective – where the largest risk inherent to the purchase tends to be the price.

In the B2B segment, risks associated with purchase decisions are much broader and deeper. They consider other related factors such as:

- Man-hours for identifying, evaluating and implementing the solution
- Potential effects on the prospect's operations if the solution fails to achieve its promised results
- Perceived career risk associated with the poor decision (in large companies)
- Sunk costs
- Adverse financial effects

> **80/20 Rule of Thumb:**
> Most B2B prospects prefer...
> 80% chance of 20% improvement
> – over –
> 20% chance of 80% improvement

These risks tend to grow proportionally, based on the purchase value, relative "visibility" of the decision and other factors.

As a result, it is often found that many prospects will fall into another application of the traditional 80/20 rule - preferring an "80% chance at 20% improvement" over a "20% chance at 80% improvement".

After the trial exercise concludes, there might be a clear winner, but usually the results are either mixed or too close for clear (and risk-averting) differentiation.

This is especially true if the solutions share common elements. Thus, the decision often comes down to personal relationships between your team and the prospect's team, and the prospect's confidence in your team understanding their situation.

Relationships between your sales team and prospects will be stronger if the prospect feels:

- Your team understands their industry and the pain that your solution will address
- You have good reference accounts
- They feel that you will support them after the sale

This is one of the reasons we recommend documenting the prospect-specific value proposition with the elements we mentioned earlier as it shows that your team has a clear understanding of the prospect's situation, its dynamics and the applicability and benefits of your solution.

You often hear the sales maxim, "people buy from people!" This is even more true in the B2B realm.

Objection Handling

Objection handling is not specific to converting prospects to customers. Throughout the sales process, you will be presented with a number of questions. Some merely seek to understand aspects of your proposed solution, but others fundamentally challenge the essence of your offer.

As the prospect commits to buying a solution and focuses on the preferred vendor, the nature of the objections change. This change often correlates to increased levels of knowledge of the business pain and potential solution(s).

By now, the prospect is likely favoring one of the vendors and may be placing objections in the path of potential, competitive ones.

The Five Occurrences of "No":

Most salespeople have heard a variation of the rule that potential customers will say "no" at least five times before they say "yes".

Sometimes I believe that Marketing understands this rule better than salespeople. The whole premise of lead generation is based on the multiple attempts needed to get the contact to say "yes".

Salespeople should think about this rule every time they hear "no". They should consider what "no" means. Is the "no" merely a timing issue – not at this time, or is the "no" a conditional one – not unless you….

Salespeople will hear "no" many times during objection handling and negotiation, and will need to find ways to get to "yes".

If you have a strong solution, a good relationship with the prospect and are the preferred vendor, you are in a strong position to close the deal. Your competition is unlikely to accept this situation and will seek to understand why they are not the preferred vendor.

The prospect may give them reasons why your solution is preferred. Your competition will view this as an opportunity to handle the objection and in some way position your offering as having a "fatal weakness" which, of course, theirs will not.

If you are not the preferred vendor, the situation is reversed. You will now be the party seeking to understand why your solution is considered inferior to the competition's. Whomever is the preferred vendor, both competitors will become immersed in objection handling.

The key to objection handling and closing a deal is to identify and address the prospect's real objection. It is important to remember the *first* objection often isn't the *real* one.

Avoid either giving up because the objection is insurmountable, or equally important, avoid putting a lot of effort to solve an objection until you are confident it is the *real* one.

How then do you establish whether an objection is the real one? One way is to probe (rather than answer) an objection. You might consider the following approaches to determine how you might respond.

- Does the objection sound real or feasible?
- Is the objection substantively echoed by other members of the prospect's team?
- Seek non-confrontational clarification of an objection. If it is the real objection, the prospect will likely be able to explain it quickly in detail. If it isn't real, the prospect may hesitate or struggle to provide insights into it.
- If the prospect does hesitate, you may have to revisit the issue at a later time or with another individual.

If you can solve a stated objection, you have an opportunity to use some form of "conditional close" ("If we solve _____ [whatever the objection], will you buy our solution?").

As with all closing statements, remember to practice this close. Some salespeople are more uncomfortable closing a deal than others. To avoid hesitating at the crucial moment, it is prudent to practice your closing.

Once you have delivered the conditional close, keep quiet and listen - even though every nerve in your body will demand that you speak. A conditional close is an excellent way to establish true objections.

The end of objection handling usually occurs when the prospect has finally decided which solution to purchase. Assuming that you are the preferred vendor, the sale will enter the "negotiation and contractual" phase at this point.

Negotiating

Negotiation is a process where parties find agreement and close the deal by trading concessions. Negotiation is a very important topic. Thus, we included this general discussion for those who haven't received any formal training.

This is not intended as an in-depth reference on negotiation - rather a few tips and techniques to lend perspective and help close the deal.

The potential buying company has decided that they want your solution, and you want to sell the solution at a price which gives you a profit. Both parties then have a common goal; namely to reach agreement on the following aspects of the deal – price, terms, conditions, deliverables, services, warranty, etc.

In a corporate buying environment, you will frequently have to work with new players to negotiate and finalize the deal, a purchasing agent (pricing) and possibly someone to address contractual issues (sale terms and conditions) – assuming these people weren't part of the prospect's buying group to begin with.

You may be meeting these people for the first time and hence may not have a relationship with them. Although you are the preferred vendor, things can still go wrong with the negotiation. It is important therefore, to handle the negotiation as diligently as you have the rest of the sale.

Sometimes the people you deal with are trained negotiators. This is actually a positive thing. It means they understand the process and everyone has a common requirement to do the deal.

PREPARING TO NEGOTIATE

Preparation is an important requirement to maximize the chances of a successful negotiation. There are a number of questions that should be considered prior to negotiating.

- Why are you negotiating?
- What are your objectives?
  - In priority order
  - "Must have" vs. "would like"
- What might theirs be?
  - In priority order
  - "Must have" vs. "would like"
- What are you prepared to trade? What are they?
- How important are their concessions to you?
- Importance of the deal? Is it too important?
- Deal time scales? Is it too quick?

This preparation is even more important if there are others from your company present at the meeting. Unless all the players on your team understand their role and their contribution, then things can go wrong very quickly.

I'm sure that you've attended a meeting where one party has disagreed amongst themselves and thereby ruined their chances of negotiating the best deal.

Your champion has a budget and wants your solution. You, together with the prospect's legal and procurement teams, need to make this happen.

Given this common goal, negotiation can be viewed as a team sport albeit with the participants playing for their own teams while at the same time considering how the overall game is progressing.

Both parties need to reach an agreement so that both can achieve their goal – finalizing the terms and conditions of the sale. The process by which the parties reach this agreement is the art (really the science) of negotiating.

The beginning point for any negotiation is two negotiators who, not only want to reach agreement, but who both have the authority to do the deal. It is likely that the main item in a buying negotiation is price, but there are other items that can be traded as concessions to the other party.

The buyer wants the lowest reasonable price, but also wants other items in the deal – longer payment terms, money-back guarantee, free installation, free training, to name some obvious ones.

The seller conversely wants the highest reasonable price but also wants other items – customer case studies, pre-purchased service agreements, Marketing assistance, and customer advocacy. With this list of "must haves" and "would likes" the trading can begin. "I'll give you this if you give me that."

In the event that the negotiation is protracted, it is a good idea to keep your prospect engaged and aware of the progress being made. In order to maintain momentum, keep this person focused beyond the sale.

Discuss any critical dates relevant to the implementation of your solution (key milestones, prospect deadlines, etc.) This dialogue helps cement your relationship with the soon-to-be customer.

Negotiating Price

Let's look at the main part of the buying negotiation – price. There are usually two extremes in the price range where both parties might settle.

The lower extreme is the one which is very attractive to the buyer but not attractive to the seller. At the other extreme, the high price is perfect for the seller, but it is prohibitively expensive for the buyer.

How then do both parties reach agreement? One party begins the bidding and the other party offers a counter proposal. The parties then normally move upwards (the buyer) and downwards (the seller) until agreement is reached.

Price concessions typically follow a staircase framework where similar increases and reductions in price lead the negotiators to a mid-point between the opening bids.

For example, if the seller offers an opening price of $50,000 and the buyer counters with $20,000 then the deal (if it occurs) will be somewhere around $35,000.

OPENING BIDS & CONCESSIONS

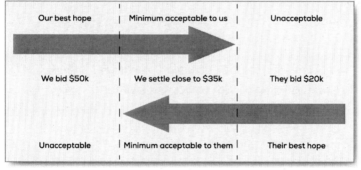

Knowing this, one party can manipulate the first counter offer as long as the other party makes the first offer. If the seller suggests $40,000 and the buyer wants to pay $30,000, then a counter offer by the buyer of $20,000 will help the buyer achieve the $30,000 goal.

This tactic of waiting for the other party to make the first concession is the first of five rules of negotiating.

1. The party which offers the first concession is usually least successful.

2. The more successful party usually has the highest expectation.

3. The person who speaks first sets the tone of the negotiation.

4. The person who asks the most questions determines the content and direction of negotiations.

5. People do things for their own reasons - not yours.

By following these rules, you not only have the best chance of achieving the goal of reaching a compromise, but also of achieving one where you have secured your "must haves" and some of your "would likes".

If your negotiating partner also feels this way, then you have a "win-win" deal. Both parties may have negotiated this deal by:

- Agreeing the desired outcome with wins for both parties
- Identifying issues/differences and tackling the easy to solve one's first
- Rewarding positive moves from both sides, with concessions of their own

There are however other possible outcomes besides win-win. These are:

- You win, they lose
- You lose, they win
- Deadlock - nobody wins

"You win, they lose"

If you "hold all the aces" during the negotiation, then you are likely to get all of your "must haves" and many of your "would likes". In contrast, the prospect's negotiator struggles to get their must haves.

There are a number of reasons why this may occur. One such situation arises when the buyer must purchase your product in order to fulfill a contract from one of your other customers. This fact, when known by both parties, leads to a deal on your terms.

If you are faced with this case, you should:

- State your "must haves" and the consequences of you not getting them.

- Release small concessions so that the prospect's negotiator can save face.

In the case where the buyer must purchase from you to fulfill a contract, keep stressing this point in a non-aggressive manner. And once this is acknowledged, allow the buyer's negotiator some form of concession.

Remember that next time you negotiate with this individual, you may be the person without the aces (i.e. the situation may be that you lose and they win).

"You lose, they win"

There are plenty of examples of these scenarios and you've probably been in a similar situation at one time or another. This scenario can occur when you are selling a commodity product with a number of similar competitors.

In this situation, you may be forced to sell at a price which seriously reduces your margins. Another example may arise because you need a fast deal to register the sale within a certain accounting period. When faced with a "you lose, they win" situation:

- Seek to understand why they refuse your "must have" concession(s).

- Try and find any consequences to the other side in not doing a deal with you.

This is a difficult negotiation if the buyer has the option of buying the similar solution from your competitor. Be careful, however, how much you concede because this negotiation may set the format of later negotiations.

"Deadlock - nobody wins"

The last possible negotiating outcome is deadlock. This can occur for a variety of reasons, but the majority of them are caused by the negotiators directly. Remember first and foremost, both parties have a responsibility to try to reach an agreement.

In the negotiation, the buying company wants your product and you want to sell. How do you get from this position to one of deadlock? This is usually caused by one or both parties not following the rules and/or making unreasonable demands on the other party.

One party then becomes emotional and negotiations spiral out of control. If you find yourself in this position:

- Don't provoke/get angry

- Support the other person's right to feel that way even if you don't agree

- Ask questions

- Seek new variables

- Be positive

- Don't interrupt/listen carefully

- Offer concessions which have limited cost/high perceived value

Marketing's Role Converting Prospects to Customers

Although Marketing has identified contacts and helped qualify potential leads, the closing the sale portion of the sales process is driven primarily by the Sales team and Sales management. Marketing moves to a more supportive role at this phase.

In this phase, Sales will most likely need marketing assistance, both to help mitigating prospects' perceived risk of selecting our solution and help differentiate our solution from competitive ones.

To support Sales' efforts, most of what Marketing will need to supply are support materials for the Sales team – likely organized in a manner that mimics how the Sales team is organized (by industry, region, product type, etc.).

These support materials can range from highly-general print collateral (brochures, sell sheets, etc.) to more specific case studies of your solution being successfully implemented in other situations that share similarities with the prospect's.

Marketing may even be asked to create highly-customized materials specific to a particular prospect that help communicate the value proposition and other important information (implementation roadmap, graphic illustration of how the process solves the prospect's challenges, etc.).

In order to accomplish this, marketers must be able to understand their buying audience and be able to anticipate at least a portion of their potential needs, wants, perceived risks, and resultant fears.

Even though Sales owns the relationship and dialog with prospects and customers, marketing management still need feedback from the field about messaging, value proposition and materials commonly needed to help salespeople convert prospects into customers.

It is very important that Sales and Marketing maintain a constant communication to ensure the effectiveness of current marketing tools as well as the need for additional or updated material and messages.

Savvy managers from both Sales and Marketing groups will realize priorities for marketing resources must strike a balance between the needs of the Sales team during these later stages and the need to keep filling the front end of the sales process with new contacts and leads.

Chapter 10: Turning Customers to Advocates

Congratulations! You now have a new customer. This new customer can serve as a gateway to future opportunities, provided they receive the benefits and value promised during the sales process.

This includes repeat sales, sales into additional areas within their organization, and even sales into other companies.

However, as you and your team are likely feeling upbeat and exhilarated about this situation, your new customer's feelings likely contrast with yours.

> **IMPORTANT:**
> Feelings after a major purchase...
> Sellers = Confident + Exuberant
> Buyers = Uncertain + Apprehensive

For your customer, it is potentially a time for anxiety. As mentioned earlier, your new customer has taken on a measure of both personal and organizational risk, by selecting your solution over others.

They did their best to select a solution to address their pain by investing "man hours" and resources into the research, review, recommendation, and commitment to purchase and implement your solution.

This is often a very "public" process and now their reputation is on the line, especially if there was resistance or apprehension with the final decision.

The selection of your solution needs to be a successful one for your supporter(s) within the customer organization. Your new partnership with your customer will now be tested.

While you ultimately want the customer to be a source of future orders, they will be incapable of even considering future orders (read: added risk) until the current decision has generated the benefits promised in your value proposition.

How your solution performs against the value proposition, and how your team reacts with assistance to ensure your solution's success, will determine whether you will even get the opportunity to be considered for repeat or *additional* business.

Needless to say, this initial performance period is crucial and should often start with a candid customer dialog that revisits and reconfirms the key points of the solution, and expectations for success:

- Overall issues (pain points) and their causes
- Implications (costs, risks, inefficiencies, etc.) of status quo
- Selected solution and expected costs
- Expected benefits to be realized with your solution
- Overall expected ROI (or other central benefit)

If these points seem to echo the value proposition document from Chapter 9, this is by design. The overall intent of the dialog is to manage expectations by reminding the customer (and in some cases your own team) of what will be considered success for your solution.

You do not want to be grading your solution against criteria that may have changed without your knowledge during the period between selection and implementation.

This discussion can be very brief, but it also helps ensure that everyone is working to achieve the same benchmarks. This is especially important when the time period between the decision to purchase and initial implementation has been extended due to prolonged negotiations, holiday breaks, etc.

Get paid for successful implementations
When we talk about successful implementations, do not assume that we mean "free" installations.

As long as the implementation/installation costs are transparently part of the proposal and the order, customers will expect to pay for the service. Both parties benefit from successful installations, and the costs should be factored into the ROI.

I worked with a salesperson to close a large deal with an energy utility. Part of the deal added a full-time engineer for a 2-year period. It was hard to see why the engineer was needed for the whole period, but the customer insisted and paid for the time.

The customer's vision was to use the engineer as an ambassador to grow our product footprint into sister departments within the energy utility, and thereby, increase the influence he had over overall engineering policy.

We had an advocate with a vision who, rather than relying on us to drive advocacy alone, was prepared to invest in making it happen.

Revisiting the customer dialogue will help identify unanticipated or unseen shifts from the customer perspective.

Having reaffirmed the success criteria, you can begin working with your customer to achieve a successful implementation.

The partnership between your, and your customer's team will strengthen the relationship and likely ensure that the customer becomes, not only a buyer of your products, but a committed advocate of your solutions and your overall organization.

What is advocacy?

For our purposes, advocacy is best described as, "the active participation of individuals or groups in the promotion of your offering or organization".

This can be within the advocate's organization (different departments, subsidiaries, etc.), in related organizations (industry groups, your customer's suppliers and their customers, etc.) or even be in general, outside forums not affiliated with their company in any way.

In the broadest sense, advocacy can be targeted to influence different groups:

- *Organizations*: advocacy to individuals within a specific organization (internal or external).

- *Group/industry*: advocacy to specific groups sharing a common theme or industry (user groups, professional or technical groups, trade organizations, causes, etc.)

- *Broadcast*: advocacy to the general public (or audience broader than a particular industry).

In the most common model, advocacy comes from users of your solution who derive benefits through its use.

Under certain circumstances, advocacy may also include non-customers. These non-customers may recognize your product's value, and may even promote it, but they may not have a need to buy it.

Non-customer advocates typically range from opinion leaders in a certain industry, to spokespeople who are paid to publicly endorse, or advocate for your company or offering.

While there are often opportunities to pay opinion leaders, experts, and even celebrities, to publicly advocate for your product or organization, the most credible source of advocacy is your customer base.

Why customer advocacy?

There are two direct sales-related benefits to be gained by working with customers to develop advocacy.

1. *Internal to customer*: advocacy within your customer's organization to help grow their overall investment in your products

2. *External to customer*: advocacy of customer outside their organization to help you penetrate new customer organizations

In order to grow from your initial sale, you need to retain your status of being the customer's preferred vendor within the offering category you represent.

It is very hard to grow from the initial order if you are under attack from your competition, or if your offering is failing to fulfill expectations. There are important factors which pose challenges for companies to maintain or protect their "preferred supplier" status.

In a commodity situation, customers tend to be more open to alternative solutions due to a perceived lack of difference between them.

While you may have managed to use this to your advantage during the sales process to unseat a rival, it can just as easily be turned against you once your offering is now the solution of choice. This lack of perceived differentiation and resultant commoditization ultimately manifests itself in terms of price competition.

Additionally, the lack of perceived difference between potential solutions, also enables your customer an opportunity to "shop around". This is especially true if your solution is not exceeding every expectation.

Under these circumstances, the receipt of an offer for an equivalent solution at a lower price, where resultant savings would be greater than the cost to change from your offering, becomes very compelling.

The differentiation of your offering (which you hopefully gained during the sales process) must be maintained, or even grown after the sale, to ensure that your offering is not displaced by a competitive one. This occurs more often than one might think, especially after companies close a sale, take the newly-closed business for granted, and move on to the next opportunity.

It is incumbent on both Sales and Marketing groups to help ensure that customer satisfaction is fulfilled, your offering is living up to expectations, and differentiation is maintained. Customer advocacy can only be generated once these conditions are met. They are not guarantees that it will happen, but their absence thwarts its development.

Another important factor to consider, is the ease with which customers can get information and compare products in today's connected world.

If you provide an "off-the-shelf" offering in a populated and commoditized category, a head-to-head comparison of your offering versus your competitors, is at your customers' fingertips.

And if that comparison was not generated, or at least guided by your organization, rest assured, it does not favor what you have to offer.

Though seemingly counterintuitive, it is in this environment that ongoing dialog and relationships with your customers matters the most. You gain (or at least protect) business by making sure your customers feel valued, and that they view you as a trusted partner, rather than merely a supplier.

Though your offerings may be similar to competitors', the impression of your customers that they are doing business with a team vested in their success, will move the point of differentiation, from the offering itself, to the team or individual who is providing it.

Organizations that focus and invest in relationships between their employees, customers, and partners, consistently outperform their competition. The pinnacle of this relationship is reached when you convert customers from being "passive" about your offering (i.e. just buying it) into "active" advocates for you (i.e. promoting or recommending you) to both internal and external parties.

Advocacy Internal to the Customer Organization

Advocacy by a customer within their organization is important because we have, over several years and in multiple organizations, observed that the traditional 80/20 rule often applies to revenue - roughly 80% of a company's revenue is generated from 20% of their customer base.

Over a more extended period, say 3-7 years, the 80/20 rule still applies, but the 20% of customers responsible for the 80% of your revenue, are generally not new customers, but are your prolific repeat ones.

These customers purchase from you several times a year, and/or, expand the penetration of your offerings within their organization.

Furthermore, extending the timeline to 8-10 years, the revenue from existing customers can amount to 10, 20 or even 30 times more than their initial first order.

> **Another 80/20 Rule of Thumb...**
> Roughly 80% of a company's revenue often
> – comes from –
> Just 20% of their customer base.

Another reason it is important to create and leverage internal advocacy, is the required resources it takes to sell to existing customer versus acquiring new customers. In almost any setting, it usually takes less time and cost to sell within an existing customer.

Existing customers are already prequalified, and many of the administrative processes required to close a sale with that organization, have already been addressed by your first sale or transaction with them. This is especially pronounced in high-cost, consultative or technical environments where the purchase is considered long-term and/or high-risk.

On the value communication side, your success with your current customer advocate helps to mitigate perceived risk.

Your advocates can help clarify your offering, provide insights into its application and help communicate its value to their associates - using metrics that are already recognized within the company.

From the administrative side, your customer's purchase process may have involved the vetting of your company, and sign-off approvals from multiple groups.

As you proceed through the new sale with the new group, it's likely that much of the purchase process will be common with those of the first sale.

This will mean that these time- and resource-consuming steps will not need to be repeated, and the amount of time to close an additional sale will be reduced.

In addition to having potential to buy from you several times and advocate for you within their company, customers can also recommend your products to other companies to help you acquire new customers.

Approving New Vendors...

The process of agreeing purchasing terms and conditions, approving, and entering new vendors into the purchasing system is not a trivial activity for larger companies. Many larger organizations subcontract the purchasing function to third parties for any deal below a certain size.

Consider a situation where you are approved as a direct vendor, and its advantages for securing repeat business. When working at a previous company, we benefitted from this advantage when selling to a large industrial company. We were a very established vendor of this company and we had great advocates in a number of their engineering divisions. We had negotiated a contract which made buying from us relatively easy.

Another division, which didn't use our product, found a better solution for their needs. They began the process of purchasing this product from our competitor. Once the approval process reached a level beyond the divisional one, questions were asked about why the division was proposing to buy a non-approved product, when they could buy a product already approved.

Logically, the choice by the new division to buy from our competitor was a good one, but they couldn't find a supporter to add the new supplier to the vendor list.

Ultimately, the new division gave up on the competitive product and purchased our solution using the terms and conditions of our corporate umbrella contract. Our advocates made it easier to buy from us and in doing so kept our competitor out of the account.

Advocacy External to the Customer Organization

Under certain conditions, it is possible for customers to advocate for you outside of their organization. Though they will typically not be able to advocate with an organization that is competitive to theirs.

External advocacy often takes on more of a "public" or "broadcast" type of form instead of a more direct and personal approach.

This external advocacy can take on a number of different forms, but some of the most common include:

- Public endorsements or quotes

- Case studies or presentations at industry (or technical) events or forums

- Authored white papers or other promotional materials

- Positive online reviews (social media, online buying outlets, etc.)

This type of advocacy is more geared to supporting the acquisition of new customers than repeat customers. Though this does not have the same "direct" effect on sales as personal advocacy, it can play a large role supporting your efforts to attract, identify and even qualify new customers.

Advocacy plays a significant role from a marketing perspective, in terms of attracting and identifying new customers by providing substance and credence to marketing messages.

Advocacy provides an indirect method for a potential customer to see how your offering is applied in situations like their own.

This allows potential customers to determine whether to include your offering in their "solution set" for further investigation. Clearly, the more advocates with their success stories your company can use, the more likely you will find an advocate which is a good match for any potential customer.

Whether the delivery mechanism for this advocacy is something as broad as a website, or as targeted as a specific case study provided to a lead to help with qualification, external advocates can provide significant value to both your sales and marketing efforts.

Tertiary Benefits of Advocacy

In addition to sales and sales-focused marketing, advocacy can offer other intangible benefits. Some of these include involving your customer advocates across disciplines.

- *Product development*: gaining candid insight in terms of strengths, weaknesses and potential improvements to your offering and comparisons with your competitors offer. In certain technological scenarios, collaborative efforts in terms of actual product development between customer and vendor, benefit both parties and further buttress your relationship.

- *Marketing Research*: participation in focus groups, surveys and other activities intended to better understand customer challenges, purchase motives, messaging, critical attributes and their priority, etc.

Though these benefits are labeled as tertiary, they can be just as important as the internal and external applications of advocacy - depending on the nature of your organization, offering and overall market.

While advocacy offers great value in all these roles, there are certain conditions needed within your organization to cultivate it.

What business culture is needed to create advocacy?

Great service is key in the early stages of the relationship. But over a longer term, the relationship between you and your customers is built around the value you drive through your overall offering.

Your attempts to develop customer advocates will not be successful if siloed as part of the sales process. It must be more than just a program within your company. It needs to be an ingrained culture which genuinely wants to make the customer successful.

Building this culture starts with sharing the value of advocates and repeat business within all levels of the organization. This includes sharing many of the advantages of advocacy and repeat business we have just discussed in this chapter.

Sales scenarios that include actual figures and percentages of repeat business, what it means to the company, as well as any employee bonuses, profit sharing and potential future raises, will help everyone in the organization better understand their value to the process and the overall organization.

Everyone should be educated about their influence over advocates, repeat customers and what this means to company revenue. This can involve examining job descriptions to determine areas of customer influence and establishing customer-centric practices.

Even if employees do not directly contact the customer, they are more likely to perform their jobs with the customer in mind, once they understand that they do make a difference helping Sales and Marketing develop advocacy.

This culture needs to be enacted across all levels of your company, with management leading by example. Through management's example, employees need to understand that the company thrives when it solves customer problems. It should filter through the organization down to those that provide day-to-day contact and support of your customer, and to the receptionist who answers inbound phone calls.

In this way, advocacy ensures your revenue growth by sharing an understanding of your customer base, its business, building strong relationships, and supporting customers to ensure their ongoing success by doing business with your organization.

Role of Sales in Building Advocacy

Though isolating your advocacy in the sales process can be detrimental, it is Sales and Marketing who must spearhead the effort from an organizational point of view, with the rest of the organization providing either direct or indirect support for these efforts.

As we discussed in Chapter 5, the traditional funnel views a salesperson primarily as a hunter winning new customers.

Hunters play a very important role in all companies and are especially important in startups. But once the hunter wins a new account, they need to switch to more of a farmer mentality to nurture the account for repeat sales and create advocacy over the long term.

Farmers play a significant role in companies where a growing percentage of business is coming from existing customers. Others within your organization will play their part in developing advocacy, but the farmer is both a relationship builder and business advisor to your customer - constantly seeking to eliminate the customer's pain by selling more of your solutions.

Typically, farmers are motivated to:

- Get the customer to buy more.
- Get the customer to buy more often.
- Get the customer to place larger orders.
- Get the customer to recommend you.

As hunters win new customers, the farming role becomes one of growing revenue by nurturing and growing these new customers and identifying opportunities to generate "add on" business. Farmers ensure the relationship with the customer is a strong one, and by doing so, they generate customer advocacy. As discussed earlier, this advocacy can help the company grow business both inside and outside their company.

How does a salesperson work with a customer who has the potential to make multiple purchases over a number of years? The key is the relationship with the new customer – keep it personal.

Salespeople should meet with new customers on a regular basis. These meetings provide the salesperson with opportunities to learn more about the customer, their industry and additional challenges (or product uses) that may not have been uncovered as part of the sales process. A good farmer should be able to give both their customer's elevator pitch, as well as one which outlines the benefits the customer realizes by their use of their products.

When possible, salespeople should encourage a number of customers to meet and share experiences and best practices. The customers should have some overlap or similarities in the application (or use) of your solution.

In certain situations, different salespeople on your team may need to coordinate with each other to ensure that as many applicable customers are included in these events as possible.

These meetings often include user or industry groups, technical or advisory committees, or any other sort of forum for dialog. Whatever the forum, positive discussion surrounding the use of your products tends to foster advocacy.

It is very important that salespeople document important points and outcomes of all customer meetings. (Savvy marketers will also want a level of involvement in this as well to support their own role in this process, but we'll discuss that shortly.)

Ideally, these reports provide the basis for account plans with initiatives where the customer is provided with compelling reasons to further invest in your products.

As both parties grow the relationship, new "pains" (i.e. opportunities) will be discovered, and you will be in a position to expand your value propositions to win new proposals and grow your sales.

Marketing's role in advocacy

Since Sales owns the relationship with customers, they will likely be the most hands-on during interactions with customers to build advocacy.

While Sales farmers will likely be focused on advocacy for repeat and added business with the same customer, Marketing's role in advocacy development is two-fold – facilitate dialog and learning more about the customer base.

This best equips the organization and salespeople to attract and develop new customers (indirectly supporting Sales' efforts to "farm" existing customers as well).

Facilitate Customer Dialog

Marketing's first and primary role is to facilitate ongoing, candid dialog between your organization and customers.

This is frequently accomplished by creating strategic touch points to connect with customers outside the realm of contact for day-to-day activities (i.e. technical support, credit department, etc.).

The possibilities for these connections is wide and varied depending upon the short- and long-term needs for your organization. These connections can be broad, such as an automated customer-wide survey or newsletter.

They can also be focused, such as approaching a specific customer about referrals, developing a case study or providing general endorsement quotes you can use for promotion among new customers.

Marketing can also target a subset of the broader customer base. One example might include working with focus groups to develop industry presentations or even developing a formal program to motivate customers to give you highly-positive online reviews.

Your selection of outreach to create the necessary touch points for your advocacy program should reflect the attributes of your customer base, their typical interests relative to your offering, and what you are looking to accomplish or obtain as a result of your outreach.

For instance, if you are looking for general endorsements or quotes, your immediate needs may be better addressed by a user group panel in a guided discussion, designed to elicit the types of responses you need to document.

If the goal is to identify ways to improve or add features to your offering, a guided focus group of customers (and maybe non-customers) may be your best bet.

If you are looking to become more visible to potential customers, a program designed to motivate customers to author positive online reviews might be a good fit. The product(s) of these efforts can then be used by Marketing as messaging and content for your outbound promotional activity as well as your response infrastructure.

The key to any effective advocacy program is identifying motive(s) that will make your customer want to spend the time and effort to advocate on your behalf.

In certain cases, there may also be an element of risk to being an advocate for your organization or your offering, since your advocates metaphorically attach their name to your organization. Thus, if your organization fails to deliver on promises made to customers where an advocate was involved, there is risk their reputation could experience some adverse consequences.

As such, you must identify what would motivate your customer, on an individual or aggregate level, to be your advocate and incorporate that into your advocacy efforts. Advocacy that is less effort tends to require less in terms of motivating factors, while higher effort endeavors will require more overt motivation.

For instance, short and positive online reviews from your customers are relatively low effort and often the opportunity to voice an opinion is motive enough for action (see Amazon®, TripAdvisor®, etc.).

In contrast, a high-effort activity like a customer-written technical paper may require a more overt motivator. It may be necessary to offer future discounts or active promotion of that paper within its industry to improve the visibility and status of the author.

Different industries and different levels of commitment will largely drive the type(s) of motivation necessary for advocacy.

As you can imagine, there are a myriad of options for Marketing to motivate and create touch points with your customer base. But it is highly-recommended that Marketing either brainstorm or at least involve Sales in the early stages of these outreach efforts.

Since Sales is likely acquainted with the customer base at a personal level, they are best suited to provide initial direction in terms of the most effective outreach that will support their farming efforts and how this information might overlap and serve Marketing's objectives as well.

Learn More about Your Customer Base

Facilitated by creating touch points for customer dialog, Marketing's second role for developing advocacy is to learn more about the customer base. Marketing owns the barometer to track the customers' views, and the obligation to represent the "voice of customer" in certain internal functions (product development, marketing message creation, etc.).

While salespeople sometimes claim they know all there is to know about their customers, the customer is often more comfortable expressing opinions and giving feedback to marketers rather than salespeople, technical people or others with whom they have daily contact. This may be due to the perception that marketers will be using their feedback for purposes other than to "upsell" to them.

Either way, marketers should be taking advantage of the contact points to learn all they can about the customer base, their challenges, research methods, information sources, purchase criteria, motives, perceived competitors, and other dynamics that affect the purchase process from either side.

This customer information and ability of Marketing to accurately represent the voice of the customer is of massive value throughout the organization, especially among product development and sales teams.

Even if salespeople are not involved in the touchpoints that uncover this customer information, this input will be crucial to their efforts farming business from the existing customer base.

It will also offer similar value for sales teams as they develop new customers that share similarities with current customers. A better understanding of current customers that enables your sales team to draw conclusions about those currently in the sales process, can only be an asset to your efforts.

For its own purposes, a thorough customer understanding also enables Marketing to be more effective at developing marketing plans and messages.

Understanding how your target audience thinks, what they feel, and where they gather information, is of enormous value when crafting messaging and planning for outbound communications and inbound infrastructure.

Advocacy as Part of Your Sales Process

Referring to the overall sales process diagram outlined in Appendix B, the funneled advocacy segment is deliberately rendered so that it is larger at the bottom than it is at the top.

After reading this chapter, we hope you'll understand the reasoning behind this - new customers going into the funnel help grow future sales through advocacy and repeat business.

Chapter 11: Management of the Sales Process

Now that we have discussed our sample sales process and the implications for each of its stages, it is imperative that you have a basic understanding of key applications and tools for managing your own process.

The approaches for business planning, sales forecasting and CRM either directly use or indirectly leverage the principles and measures that can be provided via your disciplined sales process.

Using the Multiple Funnel Metaphor as a Business Planning tool

There is a considerable upside for using the multiple funnel approach when you create the sales revenue portion of your business plan. As part of your business plan, you will need to be able to predict the overall flow of contacts through your sales process in order to achieve the desired outcome of customers (i.e. revenue).

A good way to initiate the sales planning process is to start by estimating the value of sales which comes from both repeat customers and through new customers. For planning purposes, it is important to consider new departments of existing customers to be new customers.

You don't need to generate the contact if they are an existing customer, but you will often need to find the name of a contact in another department to be able to have any opportunity to sell to this person.

Once the split between new and existing customers is identified, you can estimate the number of deals needed for both existing and new customers by using an average sales value (or transaction value).

Working backwards through your sales process by using historical results and anticipated future results, you can determine conversion ratios between each of your sales process stages. These ratios enable you to forecast the number of prospects needed for each new sale whether from new or existing customers.

Unless your company is a new startup, there should already be contacts, leads and prospects (or whatever your terms for them are) populating your system, enabling you to get at least a baseline measure of your conversion ratios.

You can then continue to work backwards through your sales process using the same logic of conversion ratios to determine targets for each of your various process stages. This process is best described using the diagram below (larger version in Appendix C):

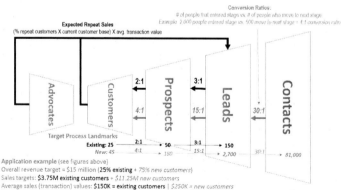

Please refer to Appendix C for a larger version of diagram.

In our example, we have calculated that we need 25 orders from our existing customers and 45 orders from companies who haven't as of yet, purchased from us. For every one of our existing customer deals, we believe we need two opportunities who will progress to become prospects.

In this illustration, we are less confident on persuading non-customer prospects to purchase, and hence we believe we need four non-customer prospects to ensure one of them will purchase from us.

This calculation continues backwards through the lead stage where we believe we need 250 leads from customers and 2,700 leads from non-customers, to meet the sales expectations. And ultimately backwards to contacts where we have a target of generating 81,000 new ones.

As your Marketing and Sales teams continue to work together, these ratios will constantly change as reality improves the accuracy of the model. Therefore, re-estimating and updating of conversion ratios must be performed routinely as part of your sales planning process.

Often a more detailed forecast may be possible if you measure the average transaction value both from existing customers, and new customers separately, since the average transition value may differ and thereby affect the accuracy of your plans.

This measure can even be distilled down to the transaction size by customer, but this will only be practical for larger customers. You will need to decide the granularity of your calculations based on your business, customer base's size, age of your relationship, and overall practicality.

Timing is another variable that must be factored into your forecasting calculations. You may need more contacts, leads, prospects in the system than the sales process model suggests, since some of these will convert outside the bounds of your organization's internal (and/or fiscal) reporting periods.

For the model to work, enough prospects, leads and contacts need to be either generated or already in the system, to meet both the needs of Sales in this period, and the ones that will slip into the next period.

Fortunately, this model can accommodate fiscal deadlines by assuming prospects, leads and contacts already in the process before the start of the period, offset the ones which will slip into the next period.

Though not perfect, this simplifies the task to one of generating enough contacts to satisfy the sales goals for each period.

As you move forward, another variable to watch is the average time it takes for individuals to convert from one stage to the next. This will give you a better understanding of the timing variables and enable you to develop more accurate sales forecasts.

Sales Forecasting

While the role of a salesperson is to close as much business as possible, they must also forecast as accurately as possible. Sales forecasts represent the best estimate of how much revenue you can generate – giving managers and executives a view of the overall business.

Accurate forecasting is essential for predicting the cash flow needed for effective planning of resources in the future. Many companies fail because their costs are set to a poorly-forecasted level of business, which fails to materialize.

Although non-Sales people may think a forecast is largely a guess at the future, the Sales Manager needs to produce an accurate forecast by aggregating the respective sales forecasts of the team. This means the manager must understand the details behind each potential sale to produce the overall forecast.

A lack of consistent interpretation of the sales stage definitions by individual salespeople is a frequent challenge for the Sales Manager. While it can be argued that the transition from a lead to a prospect can be a subjective interpretation, it is important that the accuracy of the sales forecast transcends this consideration.

Some companies attempt to overcome this by including leads and prospects in the forecast. While in theory, this might hint towards a greater level of sales forecast accuracy, in reality, it encourages the Sales team to own the lead and potentially eliminate the lead nurturing, provided by Marketing, to move the lead along the customer journey.

Should a company, then, only include prospects, or include both prospects and leads, in the forecast? There is no easy answer. Much depends on the number of transactions, the value of a typical transaction, and length of the sales cycle.

The ability of a Sales Manager to accurately forecast is usually the result of years of experience in dealing with salespeople and prospects. Unfortunately, this skill is not easily transferrable. A lay-person can look at the figures and forecast a number which is pessimistic or widely optimistic.

The accuracy of the manager's forecast depends on a number of factors: historical data, the experience level of the Sales team as well as their length of tenure with the company.

Although harder to control, the accuracy of the Sales Manager's forecast is also enhanced by a large sample size of prospects since this reduces the forecasting risk.

USEFUL FORECASTING TIP:

Improve the accuracy of your sales forecasting by tracking and internally publishing the results.

Consider the four outcomes for each salesperson's monthly, quarterly or annual forecast:

- Achieved a better result than forecast
- Achieved a poorer result than forecast
- Achieved their sales target
- Failed to meet their sales target

If you don't want to put the effort into creating a sales questionnaire, try instead to internally publish the results of each salesperson against the four outcomes.

An example might be "Jane Doe achieved 105% of her target but forecast she would achieve 180% of target."

After implementing a similar system and publishing results on a monthly basis, the authors noticed that the accuracy of reporting improved significantly without any drop-in sales achievement.

When Sales Managers ask for a forecast from their team, what are they getting? Forecasts from individual salespeople typically include three pieces of information:

- Value of the deal(s)
- Percentage probability of deal(s) closing
- "Best guess" month when deal(s) are most likely to close

While salespeople may be good at predicting the value of a deal, they tend to be less accurate when forecasting the likelihood of the deal closing, and the probable timing of the close.

Let's look at a forecast where a salesperson predicts a 75% chance of closing a deal, and where the current information suggests that the deal will close in March. This is nearly always entered into a forecast with a 75% chance of closing in March. But that may not be what the salesperson is predicting.

The salesperson may be saying that there is a 75% chance that the deal will close at some stage in the future and that at the moment their best guess is that the deal will close in March. In this situation, we have three potential sources of error:

- Accuracy of forecasting the deal at 75% chance of closing
- Accuracy that the deal will close in March
- Combined effect of both inaccuracies on the overall forecast

There is also a fourth variable in the equation - which of the salespeople is making the forecast. Two salespeople looking at the same information will likely make different predictions.

We must reduce the discrepancy introduced by different salespeople to improve the accuracy of sales forecasting and, in doing so, reduce the dependence on the Sales Manager.

To start, there are two areas of potential variability from salesperson to salesperson:

- Percentage probability of the deal closing
- "Best guess" month when the deal is most likely to close

The best way to improve the accuracy of closure probability is to create guidelines to help the salesperson complete the forecast.

This can be achieved by using an account by account questionnaire to calculate the predictive sales percentage. These questions need to be structured to capture the current status of the deal. Examples might include:

- Have we identified the recommender?
- Have we identified the decision maker?
- Do we know and understand the company's pain?
- Do we understand how the company buys products?
- Has the company committed to buying a solution?
- Have we met with the decision maker?
- Have we presented our solution?
- Have we presented a viable value proposition to the decision maker?
- Are there resources currently in place?
- Has the company decided to buy from us?
- Have we started negotiations?
- Are we awaiting the official approval/selection of our solution (PO, signed contract, etc.)?

Based on answers to these questions, percentage deal closing probabilities can be assigned. This will remove much of the forecasting variability from different salespeople. It will also enable sales management to emphasize the importance of each question in the process.

Rules can be built into the forecast to ensure that stages cannot be skipped. For example, a salesperson can be prevented from checking the box to question 10 (has the company decided to buy from us?) if they haven't checked the box to question 2 (Have we identified the decision maker?)

These different questions can also be used to drive the prediction of the closing timeframe. For example, we might create a rule which says that a deal must have answered up to at least question number 10, before it can be included in next month's forecast.

We are not suggesting you should adopt this approach verbatim. Each situation is different and will need to be addressed as such. We merely recommend that you put some logic into your forecasting process to glean more meaningful and accurate predictions from it.

Customer Relationship Management (CRM)

The number of references to CRM systems in this book provides an indication of how important a CRM system can be to the success of almost any organization.

We have consistently outlined the benefits of having a CRM system to manage your sales process relationships, their data and information.

Imagine writing down all customer interactions throughout every step of your sales cycle. This would be a very complex and almost unmanageable task.

Additionally, consider that in longer B2B sales cycles, the journey from contact to customer won't always progress in a linear fashion.

It's likely that you will need multiple touch points to get your contact to respond, contacts may go back and forth between different phases of the cycle, and there may be additional people added to the process as time progresses. The list of possible variations with one customer is very large.

So far we have only considered a single sales opportunity. If you are working on several sales opportunities, each at a different phase of the sales cycle, the amount of contact interactions increases geometrically.

Suddenly, we are talking about thousands of interactions with several people across several organizations, occurring in a short time span.

Add that there are likely multiple people on your Sales team interacting with multiple contacts, in multiple target companies and soon, you have the potential for chaos that Sales Managers will have difficulty tracking or forecasting.

The numbers alone dictate that both Sales and Marketing Managers need to find tools and methods to manage the interactions with potential, and existing customers.

Given the sheer volume of interactions and the requirement of Marketing to assist at various sales process stages, help is needed to organize the workflow through the different stages of the journey from contact to customer and onwards into advocacy.

As your number of customers grows, so does the resultant relationships and the amount of information and data that needs to be managed. This information and data needs to be shared across various teams within your own organization, especially those that deal directly with customer contacts.

This is where a CRM system becomes essential as the nerve center for your Sales and Marketing operations. Without one, you will struggle under the burgeoning volume of information and data generated by your growing business.

What is a CRM system?

CRM is a business discipline intended to achieve customer loyalty through building and maintaining high levels of customer satisfaction, thereby increasing profits and customer retention rates.

CRM systems are a technological manifestation of the CRM philosophy – designed to facilitate its implementation. A CRM system allows you to manage your sales process relationships, their data and information, and store them in a location where employees can access them. If your Sales team is remote or spend most of their time in the field, this type of system (with remote access capability) should be considered mandatory.

Several books have been dedicated to CRM systems, and since it is a very important part of sales and marketing disciplines, it warrants inclusion in this book. However, the capabilities of CRM systems change very quickly, while the principles behind them and their application to the sales process, remain relatively constant.

Thus, we will limit our discussion only to high-level principles of CRM systems. If you are interested in learning more about technical capabilities, we encourage you to read books and other information specific to each system. However, we suggest that you review this chapter first to acquire a basic understanding of applying CRM systems prior to digging into the specific details of each system.

Starting at a very high level, CRM systems all offer similar capabilities:

- Manage general information for contacts, prospects and customers
- Track the sales status of an account – lead, prospect, customer, advocate
- Store and manage account histories

- Record sales strategies – current sales opportunities, value propositions, objection handling
- Catalog account communication – phone calls, correspondence, contracts, quotes, orders, support history

Most CRM systems enable Sales and Marketing management to review information and identify some trends through aggregated reports and desktop dashboards.

Aside from sales tracking and reporting, most CRM systems offer marketers the chance to impact and track their efforts via:

- Automation and management of marketing outreach activities (emails, trade shows, etc.)
- Tracking of lead generation sources
- Measurement of online and offline marketing activities in lead-related metrics (leads created, cost per lead, etc.)
- Evaluation of marketing effectiveness based on conversion ratios within the sales process compared to the lead source

Why CRM systems?

A web search will let you discover the other, wide and varied capabilities of CRM systems.

We believe the benefits of installing a CRM system can be distilled into three areas:

- Improved interactions and communications with internal and external contacts
- Higher sales productivity via sales and marketing efficiency
- Enhanced business analytics and decision-making data

Though these areas clearly overlap in some respects, these overlaps constitute key points when we examine each area in more detail.

Improved interactions and communications with internal and external contacts

Without a CRM system, companies generally have departmental silos. Individual Sales team members manage their own processes, Marketing generates new contacts as well as outreach to current contacts, service teams manage their own customer interactions, and the finance department manage order processing.

Each of these groups generate their own discrete sets of data (notes, reports, invoices etc.) as they fulfill their job functions.

As information on a lead, prospect or customer grows, and as more people from your company interact with your potential and existing customers, sharing access to information becomes imperative. Separate Marketing, Sales, Customer Service and Finance silos impede this ability.

Lack of access to data is compounded as individuals resort to creating their own data stores or keep the information in their heads.

Under these circumstances, loss of information is inevitable as people leave your company and new team members are forced to reacquire what their predecessor failed to share.

CRM systems improve interactions and communications by:

- Managing relationships with multiple stakeholders
- Providing an intuitive, centralized system to input and review account histories and communications
- Providing metrics to enable teams to track account status throughout the sales process

Higher Sales productivity via Sales and Marketing efficiency

In addition to eliminating the information silos, CRM systems also help automate aspects of the sales process. Examples include:

- Allowing users to set up task reminders (e.g. follow-ups)
- Managing outbound marketing communications
- Recording and tracking account interactions

CRM systems also enable Sales and Marketing teams to collaborate more efficiently by providing a single, centralized venue that everyone can access and use, regardless of whether they physically sit in your offices or not.

In essence, CRM systems monitor and sequence the sales journey to allow Sales and Marketing teams to concentrate their time, efforts and other resources on activities which directly generate results, without having to expend much time tracking and managing the process itself.

Enhanced business analytics and decision-making data

Most popular CRM systems allow multiple views of the centralized data through the generation of reports and visual dashboards.

Reports can be generated using data filters to provide key, lead generation and sales progress information on individual or multiple accounts. These reports can help identify sales and marketing trends based on a variety of variables ranging from:

- Lead sources
- Phase conversion rates
- Marketing outreach effectiveness
- Sales forecasting
- Sales won and sales lost

If you want to know which customers purchased left-sided widgets in Illinois through a particular salesperson between August 21st and September 2nd, you can generate a report to tell you. If you want to compare how many leads from trade shows became customers versus leads from print advertising, you can do that too.

To a certain extent, reporting becomes limited only by the breadth of recorded data, and the imagination of the person creating the report and running the analysis.

Considerations when evaluating a CRM System to support your sales process

An automated CRM system doesn't replace the selling skills of an experienced salesperson. CRM systems help encapsulate your process of selling, thereby freeing up the salesperson to concentrate efforts on activities which generate results.

It is never recommended that data in CRM systems be micro-managed and used to "club" members of the Sales or Marketing team (or any team for that matter).

> **IMPORTANT:**
> Your mapped-out sales process must drive the selection and structure of your CRM system – *not vice versa.*

The more Sales management uses micro-level data (sales call volumes, etc.) to threaten or coerce team members, the less information the team will want to put into the system.

This will defeat the core purpose of the system and short-circuit other system benefits. While the temptation may be there for some Sales Managers, short-term gains using these methods will ultimately have negative, longer-term consequences.

A CRM system is also not your sales process. It is a technology to help track and manage your sales process. When selecting and implementing a CRM system, it is very important to select a system that can be adapted to mimic and manage your specific sales process.

Selecting and installing a CRM system and developing or modifying your sales process to fit the CRM system is most often a mistake.

Let your real world sales process and operations drive the software capabilities – not vice versa.

Since your sales process is relatively unique, you should expect some adaptation of any CRM system to be necessary. Usually, this means you need to enhance the standard CRM system to make it more reflective to your specific sales process, and thereby, more effective at managing it.

CRM systems are not as useful "out of the box" as CRM companies might lead you to believe. Expect some modification to be necessary.

CRM systems can multiply efficiency, but they can also multiply confusion and miscommunication. Before even evaluating CRM systems, you should perform an audit of your existing sales process.

As discussed elsewhere in this book, it is essential to ensure that everyone likely to use the system uses the same sales process terminology, standards, etc. Equally important, is that they fully understand and agree with the definitions to be used in the sales process.

It is strongly recommended that team-wide training for both Marketing and Sales groups on the sales process terminology, and the sales actions associated at each stage of the process, are a crucial step to a successful, CRM system implementation.

How NOT to Use a CRM System:

During the initial stages of his career, one of the authors worked for an auto parts manufacturer that used a shared CRM tool.

The owner spent many hours reviewing each contact record in the system and devoted time in each biweekly company meeting to publicly:

- Point out failures of each Salespersons' customer interactions, based on the notes they entered in the system.
- Berate them when contacts he felt were "sure to buy" based on the entries, did not purchase.

He deemed the sessions as "opportunities for learning and motivation" for the entire team.

Unfortunately, he was correct. The Sales team learned their humiliation was reduced if they withheld most information from the CRM system. They were also motivated to circulate their resumes and escape the oppressive owner.

As a result, the CRM system was woefully inaccurate, no internal candidates wanted to transfer to Sales and few Salespeople stayed at the company longer than 6 months.

Once you have agreement on your terminology and an understanding of your selling stages, you can now start your sales process audit by creating a sales process flow diagram.

This exercise will help you clarify and reinforce your existing sales process - documenting its workflow, metrics and other characteristics.

The authors do not underplay the difficulty of this exercise, but once this has been completed, you will have a comprehensive document outlining how your sales process works.

This document then becomes the benchmark against which you can compare potential CRM systems.

Ultimately, this systematic approach will enable you to select the CRM system that both fits your pre-existing process, and can be modified to manage it. The purpose is clear.

Your new or enhanced CRM system needs to mimic your sales process, to effectively track and manage it.

Given each sales process is unique, and that CRM system capabilities are constantly evolving, comparing the pros and cons of current CRM systems on the market would be rendered obsolete quickly.

But we suggest that minimum requirements for a typical system would include:

- Marketing outreach/campaign management
- Contact information management
- Contact/lead/prospect generation, scoring and tracking
- Forecasting – guidelines on account questions
- Business reporting
- Integrate capabilities with your other business systems
- Included (or added) sales automation capability to support your sales process
- An active community of third party app developers to meet your current and future needs
- System scalability
- Data import and export in common formats (for non-system reporting)

In the authors' experience, the two of these considerations that are most often neglected, are the ability to integrate with other business systems, and scalability.

Companies implementing CRM systems may not necessarily require these capabilities on the first day, but unless they consider the future needs and associated costs upfront, the expansion of the CRM system may not be feasible.

CRM systems cannot live in isolation from your other (and future) business solutions. You should be aware that as you successfully build and integrate a CRM system, that system becomes woven into the very fabric of your organization – often beyond just Sales and Marketing groups. As a result, transitioning off a poorly-chosen CRM system could have broad-reaching effects on your entire business.

Though mostly felt in Marketing and Sales, a CRM system can greatly enhance both the effectiveness and efficiency of your organization. However, the system can also multiply inefficiency and cut effectiveness if not chosen, implemented and used properly.

A CRM system's value to your organization will be mostly dependent upon how well it mimics and then manages your pre-existing sales process.

Chapter 12: Final and Parting Thoughts

Over the chapters of this book, we've covered a variety of topics, based upon a sample sales process using sample terminology.

In summation and review, it is important to remember that not all the points made in this book will apply to your specific situation and there may be others that apply that we have not discussed. Nevertheless, the following recaps some of the high-level concepts.

Our sample sales process and terms will likely not be the same as yours – and they shouldn't be.

The intent of this book is to provide you with advice, insights and some general guidelines to follow to help optimize results by aligning the efforts of your Sales and Marketing teams in an integrated sales process.

One of the biggest traps you can fall into with this and other business books, is to assume that it automatically "plugs-in" to your organization.

This is not the case with this book and almost never the case with other books, even if that's what the authors and publisher may claim.

You will get the most value from this, and other business books, if you take the principles and adapt them to your particular business, industry and organization.

This book should be viewed as merely a tool and a general guide for helping you get the most out of your sales and marketing efforts, not an Owner's Manual for them.

Be realistic and honest when outlining your sales process

The most important recommendation we can make regarding your efforts is to have a thorough and realistic understanding of your sales process.

This sales process will be primarily defined by the behaviors of your target customers. In order to understand and document this, it is important to gather candid and honest input from both Sales and Marketing management and team members.

It is crucial to bear in mind that this input should be based upon how things actually are, not how you, or your Sales and Marketing teams want them to be.

You don't want to base your entire sales and marketing process audit on a fantasy, and thereafter, be required to repeat the process once you realize that customers identify, evaluate and purchase based on their process, not yours.

Get input and buy-in from both Sales and Marketing

It is important to involve members from both groups to ensure consensus on how the process works, along with standard terminology and definitions.

A shared understanding of the process and common terminology will help eliminate potential communication gaps later. It will also enable you to gather more trustworthy and accurate information about your overall marketing and sales efforts.

Common terminology becomes the cornerstone upon which you can improve your sales process, manage it with a CRM system, and through these efforts, grow your revenue.

Growing and automating your sales and marketing efforts with commonality multiplies efficiencies – doing the same with differences in understanding multiplies inefficiencies.

As with most businesses, you will experience staff turnover, and as you grow, you will need to hire new employees. If you provide new team members with preset definitions and a common understanding of the process, you will enable them to contribute more quickly to growth. You will also prevent them creating "their own way of doing things" and creating their own silos within the company.

The Sales Process Serves as a Touchstone for All Your Marketing and Sales Activities

Once the overall sales process has been formulated and approved by Sales and Marketing management, it represents an agreed upon set of actions and procedures designed to move people from the contact phase through the customer phase, and thereby generate revenue.

> **IMPORTANT:**
> Your sales process must reflect how things actually are, not what your Sales and Marketing teams would like them to be...

It is therefore very important that the sales process serves as the touchstone for all sales and marketing activities.

Pursuing activities that are not tied directly into your sales process undermines the legitimacy and importance of the process within both teams.

The sales process should not simply be "some document that management wanted". The effort and resources spent developing the procedures will be wasted if stakeholders follow their own agendas rather than the universally agreed upon ones.

This doesn't mean that the sales process cannot be changed as individuals find better ways of handling tasks. It means that these new procedures need to be first proposed and, if agreed upon, added into the revised sales process.

Individual or departmental deviation from this approach can, if left unchecked, initiate a slow creep towards the Sales and Marketing teams going into a rogue freelancing state.

Very soon, each department (or its individuals) simply return to their own segregated agendas and individuals undertake activities based on personal preferences or ideas.

All Sales and Marketing team activities should be performed and measured against how well they fulfill a specific objective within the process.

These activities vary within the different sales process stages. At the start of the process, the focus is finding, feeding and nurturing contacts.

Activities then shift to ones which either move contacts forward through the process, or, filter them out if they do not present a valid sales opportunity.

Finally, the actions center around closing as many opportunities as possible, before activating an advocacy program designed to find, feed and nurture the next generation of contacts.

As stated in previous chapters, the level of influence over each activity will vary based upon your particular process, but most often, Marketing will have greater influence towards the beginning of the process, with that influence shifting more towards the Sales team later.

Sales Determines its Goals, Marketing Facilitates Achievement of Them

Competent and experienced Sales Managers should be well-suited to analyze sales patterns, opportunities, conversion ratios and other inputs to determine revenue potential (customers) and resultant intermediate objectives (contacts, leads, prospects) for each step of the sales process.

Talented and experienced marketers should know how to best feed the initial part of the sales process, help Sales facilitate conversions at each subsequent stage, and ultimately, help Sales close deals and build advocacy.

Savvy and committed marketers will always track their results as much as possible and challenge themselves to make the process more efficient by feeding the process in a manner that improves conversion ratios. These same marketers will strive to provide the sales team with appropriate direct selling tools to help the Sales team close as high a percentage of customers as possible.

While each of these functions is critical, it is their alignment that produces optimum sales results. This alignment is based on an understanding of the role each function plays in the process and agreement that the organization cannot be successful without both groups pulling in the same direction.

Nothing remains static – including your sales and marketing processes

No matter what your organization's offering, strategy or sales process, it is safe to assume that your market is constantly changing and you will need to change with it. Though rates of change can vary dramatically based on your market, change can be driven by a variety of factors – ranging from competitive, to scientific, or even legislative.

This change will require your Sales and Marketing teams to routinely evolve their view of their audience, sales process and tactics.

To evaluate the effectiveness of sales and marketing efforts in light of this constant change, it is critical that you measure your efforts and the results they provide.

Thorough measurement and realistic assessments will enable your team to better evaluate and evolve in a manner consistent with your market.

APPENDICES

APPENDIX A: Selling through Indirect Channels or Distributors

Though this book has largely been written from the point of view of a direct sales model, almost all of its principles can also be applied with great effect to an indirect sales model (channel, reseller, distributor, dealer, etc.).

With a direct model, a company sells its products directly to users or end customers. When engaging in indirect sales, a company uses some type of third party to sell its products. This third party could be a distributor, a reseller, a commissioned independent sales agency, retail outlets, etc.

However, before delving into how the book's principles can be applied to those selling to a reseller in a sales channel model, let's consider why an organization might choose one model over the other.

WORTH NOTING:

If you are the final link in a sales channel model that sells directly to end-customers, then the principles in this book still apply directly to your organization selling to those customers.

This chapter was written to clarify how these principles would apply to organizations selling to resellers to develop a sales channel. Many of these same principles will apply to these organizations as well, but the dynamics of the relationship will be slightly different.

For those selling to end customers at the end of the channel, the value of this chapter will be a candid look at how your upstream vendor may be evaluating you and their business with you.

In addition, it may give you some insights that may improve your ability to work more effectively with them to your mutual benefit.

The Direct Sales Model

With a direct model, a company sells its products directly to end customers (as opposed to someone who will resell them).

This approach is more common in specialized B2B (capital equipment, business space, technical equipment, etc.) than in service based B2C segments (physicians, plumbers, etc.) where the companies generally supply services, and where necessary, resell products to support the service sales.

The most common benefits for selling directly is that organizations retain greater control using this model:

- Control of the sales process
- Total control of branding/messaging
- Control of customer support and advocacy
- More control of the people who represent the company

Controlling the sales process enables the organization to have a more direct impact on the results of sales. Through good sales process management and execution, the company is able to directly interact and profile its target market - ensuring that it is selling to the right customers.

Selling to the right customers makes it more likely that they will be successful using your product which in turn, has optimum potential to translate into strong advocacy.

Understanding the target customer also helps minimize the wasted resources chasing the wrong market sector. Targeting the right market also helps prevent the company creating unprofitable variants of their offerings.

With a direct model, you have direct contact with the potential market and therefore are able to consider the implications of product variants.

Essentially, your organization controls access to your market, there is no interference from a third-party. This enables you to better control customer support, to get direct product feedback and to increase your odds of directly building advocacy.

When selling directly, it is much easier to control branding through the use of consistent marketing messaging. It also enables you to exert more control over the type of people who represent your company in terms of their background, qualifications and other pertinent skills.

Additionally, if your product is complex, highly-differentiated, or sold via a consultative selling approach, it may be difficult to find resellers willing to invest in qualified personnel and/or training, necessary to understand and represent your product in the proper manner.

Even if you find resellers committed to training and investment in their Sales team, you must weigh the resources needed to make them productive against the resources for you to develop your own team and sell directly.

This figure must also be evaluated through the lens of your offering's pricing. Your average transaction size and overall revenue must be high enough to support the resource demands of the sales force required for a direct sales model.

If the average transaction size can support a direct model, the decision to sell directly will be influenced by the level of complexity both of your offering and of the audience to which you are selling.

The Indirect Sales Model

The indirect model utilizes intermediaries (i.e. resellers) to sell your product to end customers. This is also known as a "sales channel" model.

The company sells its products to resellers who, in turn, resell them to their customer base. This approach is fairly common in specialized B2C product segments whose resellers can consist of anyone from retail chains, to independent shops, to Amazon.

In reality, consumers purchase very few products directly from the manufacturer. But services are a different story, as the person providing the service is often the same person you are purchasing it from (dentist, plumber, psychiatrist, etc.).

In contrast to the "direct model," the organization surrenders a measure of control over sales (and to some extent marketing) to its resellers. But this approach does offer some benefits as well:

- Reduced resources needed for sales team
- Access to pre-existing customer base
- Quicker penetration of markets (geographic, industry, etc.)
- Leveraging of preset purchase behavior

The biggest drawback to the indirect model is the requirement to narrow your margins to "make room" for the reseller to add their margin, while still keeping your offering price competitive.

As a result, the benefits from selling indirectly must offset this reduction in revenue. Despite this, there are a number of situations where selling through a sales channel is very beneficial.

The most common examples are when transaction sizes are small enough to dictate sales volumes that are too high for you to fund a Sales team large enough to generate the required level of volume.

Another common example is when a company wants to ramp up the coverage of a large geographic region quickly, without a large investment in direct salespeople.

This may also be linked to a scenario where your offering has broad appeal and a competitive advantage for a finite period of time or is new and complementary to a pre-existing and well-establish product category already sold via a sales channel.

When there is synergy between your products and those of your resellers, then selling through this channel can take advantage of pre-existing purchase behaviors, patterns or expectations. It may take you years to replicate the relationship your reseller already has with target customers.

Ideally, you would like to find resellers who only carry complementary products to yours and no competitive offerings (or those that could be construed as competitive). However, this is not always possible – especially if you have an offering in an established category or a commodity.

Often, viable resellers already offer competitive products, and you will compete to either replace or be offered alongside them to end customers. Though each situation is different, there are some things to bear in mind – since resellers tend to actively sell products that will benefit them most:

- Most often reseller motivation is tied to margin (not revenue) and expected volume
- Sometimes important benefits to them do not directly tie to the bottom line
- There is inherent risk for them, you must show you are prepared to mitigate it to support sales
- For resellers, your offering's end-user advantages are not nearly as important as their *ability to sell* them

As a partner to your resellers, you must offer more than a competitive offering for their customers. Your sales and marketing team must demonstrate that they can offer potential resellers marketing support, training on your sales techniques, and other tools to facilitate sales.

These resellers likely offer a number of products for resale and will only promote your product if they can be highly-effective at selling your offering to their end customers.

A company selling to international markets may also seek indirect selling partners in foreign countries. These partners offer assistance navigating the difficulties of language, local regulations and cultural issues.

In summary, the decision to sell through resellers will be influenced by:

- Transaction volumes and margin analysis
- The geographic spread of the market
- The speed at which you need to penetrate your markets
- The level of complexity for your offering

Adopting a hybrid model

Although there are solid reasons for implementing a direct or indirect strategy, companies might find that they don't easily fit into one category rather than the other.

When selling internationally, a company may wish to exercise the control provided by a direct approach in its domestic market, but need to leverage the industry experience and/or cultural expertise of resellers to establish a presence in foreign markets.

Another potential situation where a company may want the benefits of both channels is when releasing a new offering which cannot easily be sold by its existing salesforce or existing sales channel.

Here it is not uncommon for a company to continue selling one line of products through one model while selling another product through another model.

An extreme example of this would be General Electric (GE). You can buy their light bulbs at almost any retail outlet, but you can only purchase jet engines directly from them.

Whatever your reason for wanting to implement both a direct and indirect approach, careful planning needs to go into the execution of strategy. It is important to ensure that you balance the benefits of each model for each offering.

Additionally, it is crucial that your two models _never_ compete with each other to sell your offering. You do not want to end up directly competing with your resellers. Your resellers will not want that either.

As such, if you take a hybrid approach, the segregation of the two models must be along easily-distinguished lines, and the distinction must be made clear to your resellers and internal Sales teams.

This division must be considered sacrosanct, especially amongst your internal teams. To do otherwise would risk the trust of your entire reseller network and your brand across your target industries.

Sales Process Considerations for Indirect and Hybrid Models

There are a number of ways that companies can take their products to market. Though most of this book focuses on principles typically used in a direct selling model, most of these principles still apply across all models – they are just split between two distinct audiences and level of responsibility for each.

When you sell through an indirect model, your initial customer will be the reseller of your offering. Frequently, recruiting reseller candidates follows a similar process to the one followed by a company selling directly to their customers.

As noted in earlier chapters, this is just an example of processes and yours may vary based on a variety of factors.

The primary differences are in the types of criteria used for filtering and the fact that the customer in this process is not necessarily using your product. They are reselling it to their customers.

As a result, your marketing messaging to this group must reflect the benefits of being a partner with your organization in terms of distributing your offering.

Like the direct model, you will need to focus your research on potential resellers (identify the target market and generate contacts), work with the prospect reseller to determine whether the partnership makes sense (prospect qualification) and sign-up/initiate the new distributor. In this model, your new reseller partner is one of your customers.

Another difference is the roles which you and the reseller will play as part of the sales process to end customers.

Depending on the nature of your relationship, it is likely that you will have the most responsibility at the early stages of the sales process, and the reseller will have a greater responsibility towards the end of it.

Usually in this type of relationship, the manufacturer has the responsibility of marketing to the resellers' customer base to generate sales leads for the resellers to close. Marketing's activities mimic those necessary in a direct model.

The goal of building your brand awareness, differentiation and preference is a common one. But with the indirect model, the target market is the resellers' customers and prospects and the role of selling is tasked to the reseller.

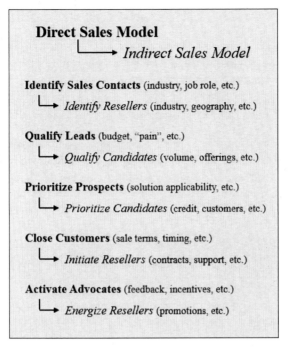

Direct Sales Model
└─→ *Indirect Sales Model*

Identify Sales Contacts (industry, job role, etc.)
└─→ *Identify Resellers* (industry, geography, etc.)

Qualify Leads (budget, "pain", etc.)
└─→ *Qualify Candidates* (volume, offerings, etc.)

Prioritize Prospects (solution applicability, etc.)
└─→ *Prioritize Candidates* (credit, customers, etc.)

Close Customers (sale terms, timing, etc.)
└─→ *Initiate Resellers* (contracts, support, etc.)

Activate Advocates (feedback, incentives, etc.)
└─→ *Energize Resellers* (promotions, etc.)

In common reseller relationships, the manufacturer drives most of the brand-, industry- or consumer-level marketing support and dictates the usage conditions for the various manifestations of their brand identity (logos, product imagery, verbiage, etc.).

Marketers know this is of critical importance for the purposes of keeping consistency across different geographies, industries and respective audiences.

When using an indirect sales model, this is one of the few areas where you must maintain marketing control. When these items are left to the discretion of individual resellers, your brand will be used in a variety of formats and manifestations – most of them not fitting with your company's strategy.

Though levels of responsibility and support provided to resellers varies dramatically based on companies, offerings, industries, audiences, and more, robust programs usually offer support ranging from initial contact generation to the stage of general support materials for identifying prospects.

Conclusion

Given the myriad of variables, advantages, disadvantages, and implications that must be considered and weighed when selecting a sales model, it is wise that managers from both Sales and Marketing groups be involved with the decision regarding the model and the plans for execution.

Both of these groups will be responsible for making your selected model a success and gaining their insights on each. The figures and estimated costs for supporting each model will be necessary to make an informed decision on the best model to adopt and on optimizing your chances of success with your chosen model.

APPENDIX B: Sample Sales Process Model

Identification
(Goal: add contacts to DB)

Sales – Profile Target
- Industry
- Job role / objectives
- Market pressures
- Purchase motives
- Pain / Value proposition

Mktg. – Message Target
- Mktg. Infrastructure
  - Website
  - Landing Pages
  - Collateral
  - Inbound call centers
- Active Comm. Outreach
  - Broadcast
  - Direct
  - Search
  - Events, etc.

Both – Address Target
- Sales and Marketing Plan
  - Repeat business
  - New business from existing customers
  - New customers
  - Sales cycle duration
- Key messages & CTA
- Activity metrics
  - Determination
  - Evaluation
- Monitor & adjust

Contacts
(Goal: identify leads)

Sales – Crystalize
- Qualify
- Tighten messages
- Priority/scoring
- Assist Mktg. with contact-generation plans

Mktg. – Filter Leads
- Position
  - Differentiate
  - Key motivators
  - Build credibility
- Tailor message to target market subset
- Mechanisms
  - Direct
  - Content
  - Events, etc.
- Call to action
- Monitor/track
- CRM

Both – Monitor
- Activity metrics
  - Determination
  - Evaluation
- Adjust as needed

Leads
(Goal: identify purchase potential)

Sales – Understand
- ID "pain", $$, process
- Solution feasibility
- Build trust
- Trust Mktg. to nurture leads

Mktg. – Nurture
- Position
  - Differentiate
  - Build credibility
- Tailor message to each target market subset
- Mechanisms
  - Direct
  - Content
  - Events, etc.
- Call to action
- Monitor/track

Both – Monitor
- Activity metrics
  - Determination
  - Evaluation
- Adjust as needed

Target Market

Potential Buyers

Qualification

Leverage

Prospects
(Goal: fit solution)

Sales – Prescribe
- Substantiate solution
  - Applicability
  - Benefits
  - Advantages
- Provider credibility
- Strengthen VP
- Objection handling
- Provide solution
- Org. charts
  - Technical buyer
  - Economic buyer

Mktg. – Mitigate Risk
- Reinforce credibility
  - Related appls.
  - Benefits rec'd
- Mechanisms
  - Content/collateral
  - Proposal support

Solution Seekers

Customers
(Goal: build on success)

Sales – Expand
- Strengthen relationships
- Different opportunities
  - Products
  - Frequency / size
  - People / depts.
- Pursue recommendation

Mktg. – Identify
- Purchase pattern(s)
  - Complimentary products
  - Buying trends
- Document results and recommendations

Purchasers

Advocates
(Goal: motivate)

Sales – Ensure Success
- Introduce technical resources
- Save decisionmaker from surprises
- Upsell / cross sell
- Get referrals

Mktg. – Facilitate
- Customer groups
- Feedback channels
- Reward programs

Catalysts

Activation   *Closure*   *Energize*

APPENDIX C: Sample Sales Process Planning Model

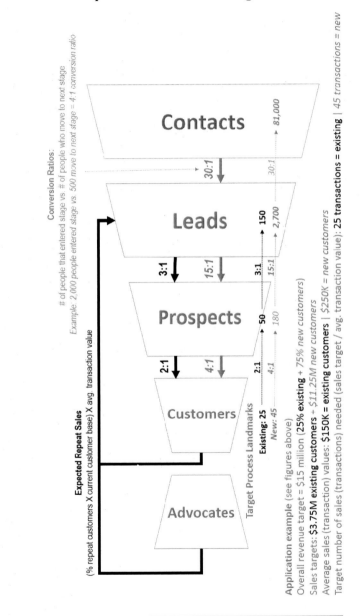

Conversion Ratios:
# of people that entered stage vs. # of people who move to next stage
Example: 2,000 people entered stage vs. 500 move to next stage = 4:1 conversion ratio

Expected Repeat Sales
(% repeat customers X current customer base) X avg. transaction value

Contacts → 81,000

30:1 | 30:1

Leads → 150 | 2,700

3:1 | 15:1 | 3:1 | 15:1

Prospects → 50 | 180

2:1 | 4:1 | 2:1 | 4:1

Customers

Existing: 25
New: 45

Target Process Landmarks

Advocates

81,000 → 2,700 → 180 | 45 transactions = new

25 transactions = existing | 45 transactions = new

Application example (see figures above)
Overall revenue target = $15 million (25% existing + 75% new customers)
Sales targets: $3.75M existing customers + $11.25M new customers
Average sales (transaction) values: $150K = existing customers | $250K = new customers
Target number of sales (transactions) needed (sales target / avg. transaction value): 25 transactions = existing | 45 transactions = new